ARTISTS' GARDENS

FROM
CLAUDE MONET
TO
JENNIFER BARTLETT

ARTISTS' GARDENS

TEXT BY
MADISON COX

PHOTOGRAPHS BY
ERICA LENNARD

Introduction by
Brooks Adams

HARRY N. ABRAMS, INC., PUBLISHERS

Editor, English-language edition: Ruth A. Peltason
Art Director: Philippe Renaud

Library of Congress Cataloging-in-Publication Data
Cox, Madison.
Artists' gardens: from Claude Monet to Jennifer Bartlett /
text by Madison Cox; photographs by Erica Lennard;
introduction by Brooks Adams.
p. cm.
ISBN 0–8109–1931–1
1. Gardens.
2. Artists—Homes and haunts.
3. Gardens—Pictorial works.
4. Artists—Homes and haunts—Pictorial works.
I. Lennard, Erica.
II. Title.
SB465.C69 1993   93–7307
712'.6—dc20   CIP

Printed and bound in Italy
by Artegrafica Silva - Parma

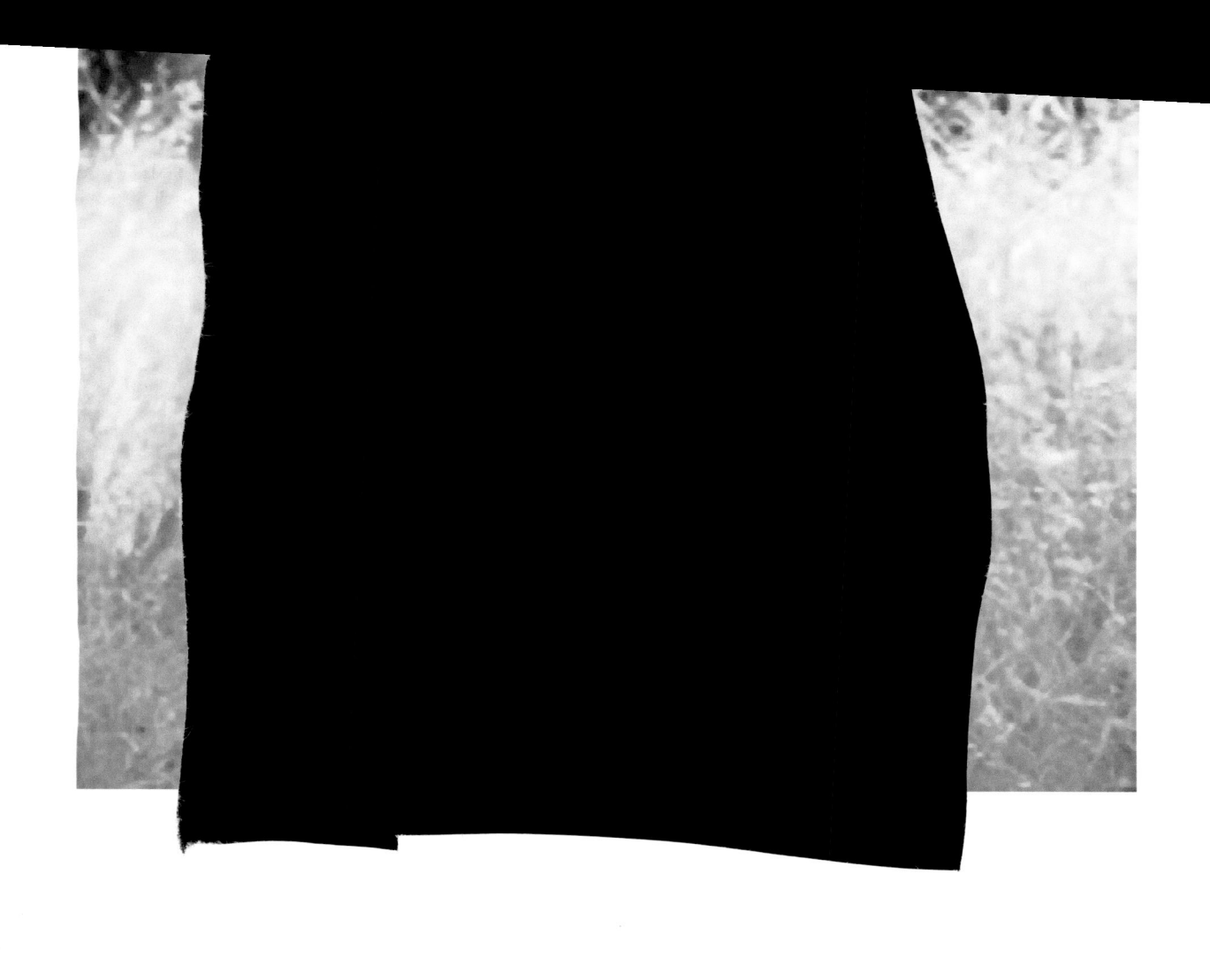

CONTENTS

ACKNOWLEDGMENTS

Madison Cox and Erica Lennard wish to extend their heartfelt thanks to the artists and those responsible for the gardens presented in this work; their generosity, kindness, and collaboration have made this book possible.

We would like to thank the following people for their help: Corinne Fossey, Philippe Renaud, William Wheeler, Dominique Rampal, Claire Desserrey, and Pierre Wittmer from Michel Aveline Editeur in Paris. We would equally like to thank Ruth Peltason of Harry N. Abrams, Inc., Helen Pratt, Tania Compton, Diane von Furstenberg, Marian McEvoy, Kazuko Oshima, Lisa Liebmann, Mary Ann Cawes, Eleanor Briggs, Atsuko Murayama, Jennifer Witbeck, Christine Khondji, Elisabeth Lennard, Katherine O'Brien, Ruth Rogers Clausen, Pierre Bergé, Mattia Bonetti, Ted Dragon, Dik Brandsma, Simon Lee, Véronique and Frédéric de Goldschmidt, Dr. Helen and Donald Meyers, Mr. and Mrs. Moritani, Mr. and Mrs. Fukiage, Shodji Sadao, Michoko Izumi, Hervé Chandes, Antonio Homem, Christopher Naylor, Jean and Irène Amic, and especially, Jennifer Bartlett and Konstantin Kakanias.

INTRODUCTION

Brooks Adams

As an alfresco studio and an Arcadian retreat, the artist's garden illuminates an individual genius and a genius of the place. In the broadest sense, the artist's garden is always a labyrinth, a journey into that person's psyche and that landscape's soul. In the most specific sense, the artist's garden is often a laboratory, a place to gather materials and test ideas. The artistically inflected landscape becomes a living book or painting, a clock or calendar that is set for the future and changes over time. Through their selections of plant materials, artists can literally reassemble the world according to their whim. The garden can be an idiosyncratic encyclopedia, a bible of personal obsessions, an ode of erudite references to older gardens, now lost and often known only through literary descriptions. Then, too, trees can be seen as living sculpture, hedges and parterres as verdant walls and floor plans, flowers as dashes of Impressionist color.

The gardens surveyed in this book swerve between Arts and Crafts impersonations of frowsy bounty (Giverny and Charleston) and Cartesian impositions of absolute, gridded clarity, be it in city gardens, for example, Joaquin Sorolla's in Madrid and Jennifer Bartlett's in New York, or bucolic retreats with ancient Pompeiian overtones, such as Betty di Robilant's

Peter Paul Rubens, Rubenshuis, Antwerp, Belgium—Rubens's garden in Antwerp reflects the most advanced garden theories imported from Italy in the early 17th century. Having returned from an eight-year sojourn in Italy in 1608, Rubens constructed a luxurious townhouse complex that included his residence, painting studios, and a large city garden. Composed of four rectangular parterres outlined by low yew hedges, the garden also contained a fountain, a pavilion dedicated to Hercules, and an arched wood pergola overplanted with honeysuckle. Renovated since 1937 when the City of Antwerp acquired the property, the garden restoration was based on Rubens's La Promenade au Jardin, which depicts the artist and his second wife walking in the finely detailed landscape.

garden near Porto Ercole, Italy. Artists are capable of the genuinely humble and understated moment, for instance Hiroshi Teshigahara's ikebana flower arrangement exhibited outside in a Japanese rock garden. Yet artists can also create omnivorous total environments, such as Niki de Saint-Phalle's Tarot garden in Tuscany, which offer Surrealist hallucinations of esoteric order, even while taking us back to the origins of the modern grotesque in such early twentieth-century gardens as Antonio Gaudí's phantasmagoric Park Güell in Barcelona.

The idea of the grotto as a birthplace for art is one that has persistently intrigued me even when, as a graduate student in art history, I chose to study the seventeenth-century activity of the Académie Royale des Beaux-Arts and willfully located its most exuberant activities in the garden of Versailles. There, particularly in the Grotto of Thetis, the original setting, now vanished, of François Girardon's *Apollo and the Nymphs*, I found the most enduring and enticing symbols for how artists wanted to imagine their sense of relation to nature and to each other. Of course, such vaunted artistic self-images could also be traced back to Elizabethan masques, often performed in gardens, and Rubensian royal entries—temporary events or Happenings—usually designed by court artists whose private fantasies of garden art were thus put at the service of the state. If Girardon's *Apollo and the Nymphs* now survives as a Romantic ruin designed by Hubert Robert, Rubens's princely testament to his own hard-won affluence lives on as a charmingly contemporary knot garden outside the Rubens House and Museum in Antwerp. In this book we note that both Gustave Caillebotte outside Paris and Jean-Charles Blais in Provence constructed their own fantasy antiquities out of old/new garden ruins. And in the realm of museums, those latter-day gatherings of the muses open to the public, we find Joan Miró's pan-Mediterranean garden at the Fondation Maeght in St.-Paul-de-Vence, Jacques Majorelle's cobalt blue garden in Marrakech (the inspiration, perhaps, for Frida Kahlo's blue-walled garden outside Mexico City), Augustus Saint-Gaudens's Aspet, a bit of classical Rome in rural New Hampshire, and Monet's Giverny, that living monument to Franco-American friendship, supported in large part by American funds.

Many of this century's great gardeners have started out as painters. Members of my generation have become increasingly aware of the canon of such consummate early twentieth-century garden artists as Gertrude Jekyll, the longtime collaborator of the British architect Edwin Lutyens, who began as a painter until her eyesight failed, and whose gardens have been rediscovered and celebrated as brilliant achievements in their own right. In Brazil, the ebullient landscape designer and horticulturalist Roberto Burle Marx has always been a painter and draftsman, beginning with his Expressionist work of the late 1920s. But it is through his painterly inflections of nature and plant materials that Burle

Preceding spread: Hubert Robert, Château Versailles, France—In direct contrast with the other garden features that make up the wooded groves at Versailles is the Bains d'Apollon, laid out in 1776 after plans by Hubert Robert, the court painter and chief garden designer to Louis XVI. Hubert Robert's great stroke was in reworking the severe classical style of the 17th century into the romantic, theatrical style of the 18th century. Where Girardon's marble grouping depicting Apollo and the nymphs had been housed originally in a free-standing pavilion, Robert created the Thetis Grotto for the sculpture, with its visions of idealized ruins, ancient temples, and abandoned overgrown gardens.

Opposite: Gustave Caillebotte, Yerres, France—A member of the artistic circle that included Renoir, Monet, Degas, and Pissarro, Caillebotte painted gardens at his own house in Petit-Gennevilliers as well as at his family's estate in Yerres. This abandoned pavilion at Yerres reflects the mid-19th-century taste for romantic follies.

Marx is universally known as the leading exponent of the modernist landscape idiom, which often includes a keen ecological advocacy to preserve the Brazilian rain forest. Closer to home, the American painter Robert Dash is well known as an abstractionist of the New York School who produces energetic canvases in the tradition of Willem de Kooning. But who could have predicted that Dash, working in the Hamptons on Long Island, would transform his seaside property into one of America's preeminent gardens—a living Abstract Expressionist canvas full of bold strokes of color and strong, bracing lines?

Although a place might be charming and freighted with memories of older art, some artists' gardens strike me as rather subservient to their paintings. The expatriate Joan Mitchell will be remembered first and foremost for her articulated abstractions, which bear the imprint of this irascible, second-generation Abstract Expressionist. Yet a knowledge of Mitchell's garden at Vétheuil changes the way we perceive her paintings, making them look more representational, more suffused with nature, more governed by a specific genius of the place, namely the sparkling northern light of the Île-de-France that also inspired Monet in the 1870s. Many of Mitchell's late canvases were specifically inspired by trees on her property, just as Renoir, working in the South of France at Les Collettes, painted the thousand-year-old olive trees on his property late in life.

Sometimes the artist's garden and painting are wildly divergent in spirit. The American expatriate John Hubbard is a good example of such a disparity. His garden at Chilcombe in Dorset, England, unfolds on a slope in a labyrinth of verdant rooms that recall the old medieval idea of the *hortus conclusus,* or enclosed place, that was commonly employed in Northern Renaissance painting as a symbol of the Virgin. Hubbard's paintings, on the other hand, are hardy Abstract Expressionist works that, while based on his own garden, reflect a modern and free-ranging spirit. Likewise, April Gornik's imaginary landscape panoramas could not be more dissimilar to her and Eric Fischl's tidy and relatively contained garden on Eastern Long Island. Often an artist's painting and gardening seem to work in counterpoint, fulfilling different impulses of chaos and order, sublime and beautiful landscape idioms.

Gardens have traditionally served as outdoor galleries for viewing sculpture. From Hadrian's Villa to Henry Moore's landscape park, artists have used the outdoors for framing and rearranging elements of classical antiquity as well as their own fragments of modern life. In Sweden, Carl Milles's stylized Deco sculptures make a strangely Hellenic foil for a Nordic landscape garden which belongs to a whole modernist revival of 1920s landscape design, including Jens Jensen's use of Nordic plant materials and Gunnar Asplund's novel design for a cemetery in a forest. On an island in Japan, the Japanese sculptor Isamu Noguchi brought rocks from all over the world to build his spare and almost savage outdoor studio, which at times recalls Japanese feudal castles with their rocky battlements. In Eastern Long Island, the Philippine-American assemblagist Alphonso Ossorio collected specimen trees on a global scale to construct a garden that has been called "the eighth wonder of the world" by the American Conifer Society. The French collaborative team of Anne and Patrick Poirier, working in Northern Italy, constructed a miniature ruin which reframes the landscape vista behind the property in terms of space and time, creating a more gargantuan

Carl Milles, Millesgården, Lidingö, Sweden—The Swedish sculptor Carl Milles purchased this property on the island of Lidingö, outside Stockholm, in 1908, the same year he first visited Rome. The influence of Italian gardens is evident: the use of terraced levels, which Milles carved out of the rocky sloped terrain; the placement of statuary throughout; and the selection of fountains and variety of plantings. Here, Milles's The Sunsinger (1926) stands as the axial focal point to the middle terrace; the granite colonnade on the right sharpens the perspective.

sense of scale and a more tangible aura of the ancient world. Near Fontainebleau, Claude and François-Xavier Lalanne use their garden as a whimsical landscape gallery for his sculpture and her decorative metalwork, which is often directly cast and sculpted from flowers in the garden.

In the Lalannes' case, the garden becomes a kind of Wagnerian *Gesamtkunstwerk*, a total work of art that is always in progress, always changing yet always expressive of their richly collaborative enterprise. So, too, the garden at Charleston in England, the country retreat of Duncan Grant and Vanessa Bell, must have originally been suffused with bacchanalian pranks and the high-flown literary sentiments of the Bloomsbury crowd, including that distinguished writer and gardener, Vita Sackville-West, and Vanessa Bell's sister Virginia Woolf. In such garden complexes, all the arts commingle with all the senses, most notably sound and smell, to produce that exalted feeling of aliveness, that sensation of reintegration with nature and with one's own nature, that so many modern artists like D. H. Lawrence have consciously sought in a spirit of political and sexual liberation.

On a personal note, I first encountered Erica Lennard's photographs of gardens in 1980 while organizing an exhibition about horticulture in art called "Gardens of Delight" at the Cooper-Hewitt Museum in New York. Lennard's black-and-white photographs of gardens— so mute, so melancholy in their static geometries—struck me as living reincarnations of Eugene Atget's classic garden photography which, at the beginning of the 1980s, was only beginning to become widely known in America. Lennard, the self-styled expatriate, was by that point almost as much of a French artist as an American one, dividing her time between Paris and New York, and later traveling all over the world in search of gardens both ancient and modern. Thus, quite unlike Atget's local documentation, Lennard's became a global vision—with India and Japan feeling almost as familiar to her as Sweden and Scotland. Now, more than a decade later, the results of her free-ranging odyssey and relentless pursuit of garden art are presented in this new book—so different in spirit from her 1982 volume *Classic Gardens*, which focused on French, Italian, and British examples, all seen with Lennard's modern, alienated, fragmented, and starkly Minimalist eye.

This photographer came of age in the 1970s, the era of earthworks. Robert Smithson, Michael Heizer, and Walter De Maria's outdoor installations in the American West must surely have influenced her developing understanding of landscape. Now *Artists' Gardens* reveals great works of garden art, such as Ian Hamilton Finlay's Little Sparta in Scotland or Alphonso Ossorio's The Creeks on Eastern Long Island which, until recently, had gone relatively unrecognized as important earthworks, substantially contributing to the languishing tradition of twentieth-century landscape art. In retrospect, we can say with some certainty that these gardens are their artists' supreme creations—the testing ground for much of their other work as well as the most fitting memorial these artists could devise to themselves within their own lifetimes.

What do all these artists' gardens offer us? Quite simply, a rare vision of harmony, so hard to come by in our late twentieth century, with its emphasis on ecological gloom. To Madison Cox, a landscape designer and eminent writer on gardens whose professional

Jean-Gabriel Domergue, Villa Fiesole, Cannes—During the 1920s Jean-Gabriel Domergue was in great demand across Europe for his light, evocative portraits. Although also active in designing theater sets, costumes, and fashion, his most lasting creation was undoubtedly the Villa Fiesole, which became the backdrop to some of the Côte d'Azur's most legendary parties. Terraced levels are linked by a system of staircases, and the abundance of stone-carved urns, statues, herms, balustrades, and fountains mirrors the artist and his wife, Odette's, preference for the grandeur of an interpreted Italian style.

collaborations with artists such as Jennifer Bartlett and David Salle make him an expert on the dynamics of artists' gardens, we are grateful for explaining so much of how these environments actually function. By recounting the specifics of garden arrangement and plant material, and by placing these living artworks in philosophical relation with the rest of an artist's oeuvre, Cox offers the specialist and amateur alike his privileged insights about gardens that, in many cases, remain in private hands. All the great horticultural traditions are represented in this tome—the "borrowed landscape" conventions of Japan, the classical villa vernacular of Italy, the picturesque garden layout in England and France, the riot of color from cottage gardens in Britain, the axial watercourses and courtyard enclosures of the Islamic world, including Morocco and Spain. With their novel uses of color and iconography, these artists' gardens alternately venerate and upset the axioms of garden tradition, making the impossible seem eminently possible, and providing new ways of looking at the world, even new visions of paradise.

Joan Miró, St.-Paul-de-Vence, France—Miró's striking bronze-and-steel sculpture La Fourche *(1963), towering over rough-hewn stone walls and surrounding pines, dominates the Provence landscape at the Fondation Maeght. Inspired by their compatriot Antonio Gaudí, Miró and fellow Catalan architect José Luis Sert incorporated organic forms in this garden setting housing many of Miró's large-scale sculptures.*

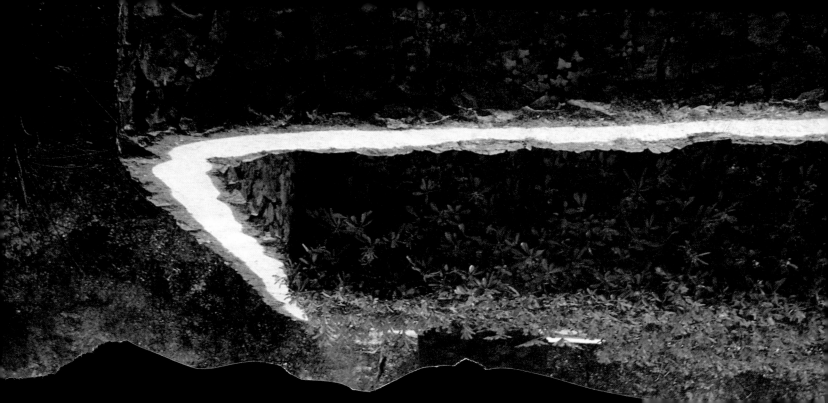

CLAUDE MONET

GIVERNY / FRANCE
1883

Opposite: A detail of one of the beds flanking the narrow gravel pathways. Rows of Iris × germanica *are underplanted with dashes of contrasting grape hyacinths and jonquils and followed by biennials, such as pansies and wallflowers,* Cheiranthus cheiri, *and* Lobelia erinus.

Most surely inspired by the many Japanese woodblocks collected by Monet, a graceful wisteria-covered wood bridge was constructed to span the two-acre pond.

Perhaps no other garden more clearly reflects the strong relationship between an artist and a cultivated enclosure than does the garden Claude Monet made at Giverny. Revered the world over, images of Monet's countryside garden situated in Normandy have become synonymous with the artist and his enthusiasm for color. Giverny is equally known to garden enthusiasts and admirers of Monet's dazzling palette. Intertwining clematis and roses, thick rows of iris, delicate wisteria clusters, or rampant nasturtiums all recall visions of a garden famous for its eccentricities, which now—nearly one hundred years later—have become standard garden vocabulary.

Yet more than the mere subject of innumerable canvases or charming photographic vignettes, Giverny portrays the characteristics of a highly individualized concept. Monet was a courageous gardener: garden conventions of the day seem to have come and gone completely unnoticed by the artist, whose real desire to learn about color and to understand light turned Giverny into a living art form. The garden was the result of, and perhaps also the reason for, Monet's art.

When Monet initially found the pink-colored house known as the Clos Normand in the village of Giverny in 1883, the garden was laid out in a typically French fashion. A central wide walk ran down the sloped site, flanked on either side by beds formed of straight and perpendicular lines. During his forty-year residence, the artist devised the planting scheme that set the garden apart from its neighboring counterparts. The utilitarian grid design of fruit tree rows and wide geometric beds became the foundation for a most unorthodox planting plan, which continues to awe and inspire today. In carrying out the geometric planting scheme, Monet concentrated massive groupings of perennials, climbing vines, and roses interplanted with seasonal annuals. Blocks of single-plant varieties were contrasted with vivid touches of other flowering plants, filling the garden with its dynamic, emotional atmosphere.

Perhaps the best-known feature of Giverny is the water garden. The bog site was created with fresh water that the artist diverted from the nearby Rû River. Existing plants in the marshy area were native iris and water lilies, to which Monet expanded to include many aquatic varieties. By contouring the pond banks and varying the plant configurations from dark, dense groupings to those that allowed for more open vista, Monet created the impression of a far larger space.

By 1892 Monet was employing five assistant gardeners, including one whose sole duty was to maintain the water, and a head gardener named Breuil. In his later life, Monet continued to add to the garden, sometimes collecting plant varieties found well outside of France. Behind every canvas depicting the garden, the neighboring haystacks, or the Cathedral of Rouen, a passion for light—and above all, for life—is evident. That continued passion produced on a site of average proportions a garden of grand and limitless dimensions.

Monet was never afraid of convention: the genius of Giverny can be found in the artist's use of simple, native plantings, such as the flowering ornamental crabapple shown here, to the more exotic water lilies that he used to stock his pond, which were gathered from all over the world.

Over the course of 30 years, the water garden grew from a small rectangular-shaped bog located behind railroad tracks across the road from Monet's house to an exotic and luxuriantly planted curvilinear water feature.

Partially concealed behind the thick, lush plantings, a perimeter path was laid out to follow the sinuous contours of the pond. Iris, large-leaved gunnera, both bush and tree form peonies, brightly colored azaleas, rhododendron, and a wisteria pergola grow along the water's edge. In the foreground are a clump of soon-to-bloom water lilies. The reflection of nearby willow trees adds to the poetic mood of the pond.

Pages 28–29: Viewed as though one were actually strolling down the lower end of the garden in late May, a succession of plantings is experienced—iris interplanted with peonies, columbines, and hollyhocks, not yet in bloom. To one side, and also in the background, roses are trained up metal hoops, painted a subtle teal color. Looming at the rear is Monet's painting studio, erected in 1914 to house his gigantic work Les Nymphéas.

Pages 30–31: For the thousands who know Giverny and the many paintings Monet made there, the curved wood bridge has come to symbolize the quintessential feature of this atmospheric garden. Two types of wisteria overhang the green-colored bridge: the white beardlike Japanese wisteria, Wisteria floribunda, and the purple Chinese wisteria, Wisteria sinensis. A thicket of bamboo crowds one end of the bridge, while the surrounding bog plants include water iris, Petasites, and a Japanese maple.

AUGUSTUS SAINT-GAUDENS

ASPET
CORNISH / NEW HAMPSHIRE
1885

Opposite: The enclosed courtyard atrium of the sculptor's gallery now houses copies of many of Saint-Gaudens's work. Framed between climbing vines is a gilded bronze replica of his Amor Caritas *plaque, which was originally exhibited at the Paris Exposition of 1900. Pink-flowering astilbe, vines, water lilies, and potted aquatic plants add a sense of intimacy to the small enclosed space.*

In 1889 Saint-Gaudens built, and redesigned again in 1904, the Doric-columned porch and trellised pergola which wraps around his studio. Along the south-facing side, a 60-foot-long perennial border of iris, hollyhocks, and later gladiolus blossom beneath the hanging tendrils of Concord grapes trained to provide summer shade.

In the final decades of the nineteenth century, America witnessed a renaissance of sorts with a great productive outburst of the arts. Classically trained architects, landscape designers, painters, and sculptors launched a stylistic crusade that shaped and formed the nearly one hundred-year-old republic with a comprehensive artistic movement that carried well into the twentieth century. Among the men and women responsible for this artistic tide was the American sculptor Augustus Saint-Gaudens.

Born in Dublin, Ireland, of a French father and an Irish mother in 1848, Saint-Gaudens was raised in New York City, where his parents had immigrated six months after his birth. Following the traditional course of the period for an aspiring artist, Saint-Gaudens apprenticed as a cameo cutter before attending the city's Cooper Institute and National Academy of Design. The twenty-year-old sculptor was a pupil at the École des Beaux-Arts in Paris from 1868 until the outbreak of the Franco-Prussian War in 1870, when he moved on to Rome. For culturally and intellectually ravenous Americans, Italy was an awe-inspiring country with its vast history and appreciation of the arts. The expatriate American communities, much like those depicted in the novels of Henry James, were composed of wealthy patrons and studious artists. Life was agreeable, inexpensive, and surrounded with a glorious history and great beauty. Among the many fellow countrymen Saint-Gaudens was to meet during his European sojourn was his future wife, Augusta Homer, as well as future benefactors and professional colleagues, including the architect Stanford White, with whom he would collaborate on many large-scale works.

Saint-Gaudens returned to America with his bride in 1874; his statue of Admiral Farragut for New York City's Madison Square Park, unveiled in 1880, brought him widespread fame and critical success. By the turn of the century, Saint-Gaudens was considered America's greatest sculptor and was made an officer of the French Legion of Honor and a member of the Institute of France. His civic monuments embellished major American cities, such as Lincoln Park in Chicago or the Shaw Memorial in Boston, while his numerous private commissions adorned the homes of the new wealthy leaders of the Gilded Age. His work fused a European classical idealism with a frank, almost rough realism and tension that characterized the energy of the emerging country's strength.

By 1885 the highly successful and financially secure thirty-seven-year-old sculptor and his family settled during the summer months in the small, rural village of Cornish, New Hampshire, where Saint-Gaudens rented a former roadside inn, known as Huggins Folly. The poetic wild landscape, with its narrow valleys, romantic glens and waterfalls, brooks and lakes was to be the sculptor's home until his death in 1907. In the final decade before 1900, the area around Cornish became a favored summer haven for scores of the Northeast Coast's artistic community, many of whom had followed Saint-Gaudens's lead. Among the New Hampshire resort crowd were those who achieved fame in related art fields and landscape architecture, including the sculptor's niece, Rose Standish Nichols, a garden designer and author; Charles Platt, the landscape architect who wrote the first American treatise on Italian gardens in 1894; and the illustrator Maxfield Parrish, whose watercolors accompanied Edith Wharton's publication in 1904 of *Italian Villas and Their Gardens.*

Saint-Gaudens's garden complex, known as Aspet, comprised a 150-acre property of forests and spectacular views of distant Mt. Ascutney and the Green Mountain range. Although the artist officially purchased the land in 1891, renaming it for his father's birthplace in the French Pyrenees, he began work on the land much earlier. In 1886 he renovated the main house, with an addition by the architect George F. Babb of an Ionic-capital colonnade and trellised pergola. A classical vocabulary of ancient Greece and Roman architecture was incorporated into all the various transformations that were carried out on the estate, including porticos and porches, balustrades, benches, and garden gates. Saint-

Against 100-year-old clipped Eastern white pines, a gilded statue of Hermes rises above the formally laid-out middle garden. Here, the geometric-shaped beds are hidden beneath the "old-fashioned" annuals and perennials that Saint-Gaudens planted to soften the straight-lined contours. The marriage of formal composition with cottage-style plantings reflected the artist's dual passion for the classical and the casual. Maintained today by the National Parks Service as the Augustus Saint-Gaudens National Historic Site and open to the public, the garden is one of the finest examples of the period in the United States.

Gaudens unified the different architectural elements and numerous outbuildings on the site by painting everything a crisp white accented in green, his two favorite colors, and with his third, a Pompeiian red, for the exterior walls of his working studio.

Much influenced by the years of study and exposure to French and Italian examples of garden composition and reflecting the then contemporary tendencies of strong architectural layout, Saint-Gaudens planted hedge enclosures of pine and hemlock as a formal framework for his garden. Employed to envelop areas and create roomlike configurations, these enclosures produced distinct atmospheres and effects. The evergreen divisions were equally utilized as scrims to screen out unwanted features or to frame particular garden aspects and distant mountain views. Within the architectural layout, Saint-Gaudens created an Italianate garden of terraces, formal beds, axial walks, fountains or reflecting pools, and copies of antique statues. The long flower borders and geometric-shaped beds were planted in a wide variety of "old-fashioned" annuals and perennials, which softened the architectonics of the formal style.

The garden is made up of three distinct parts, or levels, with the main house sitting atop the highest, or upper terrace. A series of brick steps leads down to the middle terrace, composed of formal beds and a centrally placed circular fountain. Enclosed on two sides by high hedges of sheared Eastern white pine, *Pinus strobus,* the beds are densely packed with a large collection of flowering plants that fill the garden room with a succession of seasonal bloom. Tall blue delphiniums, coral daylilies, gladiolus, and hollyhocks rise above the undulating masses of iris, snapdragons, bachelor's button, peonies, astilbe, stock, scabiosa,

*The pair of Hermes and the white-painted wooden bench with busts representing the seasons
were used as a focal point for the long perennial borders in the lower terrace garden. Tall stands
of paper birch and pine hedges enclose the room and were planted by Saint-Gaudens himself.*

and lupins. Arranged in a casual manner more in relation to neighboring heights than by
color associations, the brilliantly colorful splashes are intermixed and create a vividness of
variety and tone. A rich, velvet grass unifies the space as it does the surrounding garden
compound.

Set on axial line with the middle level are the double border and sculptor's studio of the
lower terrace. Enclosed again by dense pine hedges and a row of chalky white paper birch,
the rectangular-shaped exterior room is flanked by perennial beds edged in *Hosta sieboldii*.
Terminating the long axial perspective is a white painted wooden bench with carved female
heads representing the four seasons.

Although Aspet reflects the sculptor's reverence of a classically inspired world, it remains truly American in character and atmosphere. Bowling greens and forest walks,
swimming holes, bridal paths, and woodland picnics convey a respected kinship with nature
and the great outdoors. Interestingly enough, in relation to Aspet's European counterparts,
and with Monet's Giverny in mind, Saint-Gaudens's compound projects a simplicity of
civilized living far removed from the swelling city centers. Set in the dramatic New England
landscape of hillsides of hemlock, pine, beech, and sugar maples, Saint-Gaudens formed a
small cosmos where a zealous ardor of nature, gardens, and sport were paired with a strong
deference for the past. These converging elements were brought together by the sculptor as a
context from which has resulted a garden that embodies a distinctly American spirit.

The gilded Pan fountain, in a bed of elephant's ear, and white-painted wooden exedra are enclosed within evergreen hedges, just off the artist's studio. The grove of thick paper birch was planted in 1886 by Saint-Gaudens, as were thornless honey locust and Lombardy poplars. The two concrete end panels of the bench were carved by the sculptor's brother, Louis Saint-Gaudens.

Overleaf: Saint-Gaudens incorporated elements of classical architecture in the many transformations that he instigated at Aspet. Giant yew bushes clipped into perfect geometric spheres flank the brick steps that lead off the pergola. In the far distance is Mt. Ascutney, one of the borrowed landscape features Saint-Gaudens highlighted in his garden layout with the use of hedges, groupings of trees, or architectural elements.

PIERRE-AUGUSTE RENOIR

LES COLLETTES
CAGNES-SUR-MER / FRANCE
1907

Opposite: Nestled in protected corners surrounding the different buildings that dot Renoir's property, sudden outbursts of vegetation soften the contours with seasonal splashes of color. Here, large drifts of blue and mauve irises bloom under an olive tree; elsewhere, masses of glaucous-leaved yucca plants or the poisonous angel's trumpet, Brugmansia × candida, with its milky white trumpet-shaped flowers, provide notes of exoticism to Les Collettes.

Local lore reputes the olive trees to be over 1,000 years old, and over time many have produced hollowed cores and split trunks. Their phantasmagorical shapes fascinated Renoir, who, weather permitting, painted numerous studies of the contorted corkscrew trunks.

Pierre-Auguste Renoir, unlike his lifelong friend and fellow painter Claude Monet, is little known for his garden. These two artists, who are most closely associated with the early years of the Impressionist movement, came to settle upon two very different personal landscapes in expressing their ceaseless fascination with light and attempts to capture fleeting, momentary images. Giverny was wholly Monet's invention: the land, plantings, and color schemes were the result of his tireless attention, whereas Renoir's garden, Les Collettes, was already in existence, albeit a precarious one, when purchased by the artist. Yet for both artists, their gardens became their passion and inspiration for their work. Painting directly from nature became hallmarks of their work, with their gardens as primary subject matter.

In Renoir's Côte d'Azur garden there exists an atmosphere of soft serenity tinged with pure magic. The golden Mediterranean light is broken up, fractured, and diffused throughout the hillside property, which is caused by the towering plantings of olive, pine, and eucalyptus trees that canopy overhead. The painter purchased the farmstead in 1907 to safeguard the land after learning of its forthcoming sale, which would have resulted in the destruction of the ancient olive grove. The painter's wife, Aline Renoir, was in charge of the construction of a new house on the site; she felt the need to build a luxurious contemporary villa suitable for an artist as distinguished as her husband. As for Renoir, he claimed the remainder of the land which interested him principally and proceeded to maintain it as it had been in the past. By continuing the property's cultivated farm atmosphere of hens and chickens, grassy terraces and vegetable plots, orange trees and olive groves, Renoir preserved the land and its traditional affiliation with mankind.

Of more than 140 olive trees that existed when Renoir acquired the property, less than half survive today. Their august silhouettes overpower the sloped site with majesty and splendor. Claimed to be nearly one thousand years old according to local lore, the thick twisted trunks are crowned with rich, full canopies of silver-leafed foliage, a result of the lack of pruning over the decades. Going against the Mediterranean tradition of a severe annual pruning, Renoir preferred to allow the olives to grow in their natural, almost wild, manner. The state of neglected abandonment, or overgrown entanglement, appealed to the painter as a subject of endless study. Having been exposed to a multitude of garden styles and approaches, ranging from the formal Italian Renaissance designs he saw on trips south to numerous French examples, including Monet's Giverny, with its full-blown borders and rare water lily collection, Renoir's taste nonetheless remained for simple groupings of commonly found garden varieties. Thick beds of single-flower selections were his preference, massed together to create strong blocks of color and textural foliages. Throughout the year at Les Collettes there are numerous garden experiences, yet unlike Giverny which bursts forth in every direction from spring to fall, Renoir's garden is infinitely more nebulous and subtle, while remaining dramatic in its approach.

In the spring, great masses of bearded iris flower in dense clumps creating a vivid sea of blue, while the grassy terraces curving down the hillside become, with the seasonal rains, ribbons of bright monochromatic green. White blossoming cherry trees dot the property and enliven the bold outbursts of color. Later in the season, a long curved pathway leading up the steep hill is solidly flanked with white and pink flowering oleander shrubs, and stone retaining walls spill over in waves of brilliant reds and pinks of summer-blooming pelargoniums. The formal garden adjacent to the villa was Madame Renoir's personal domain, where she interplanted heady-scented old roses with orange trees, thereby creating a luxuriantly fragrant area. Throughout the property are old Provençal-style constructions: an ancient farmhouse and gardener's cottage, storerooms and toolsheds, all washed in a faded ocher color with red tile roofs, black wrought-iron fixtures, and pale blue wooden trim. During the years of great acclaim and international recognition, Renoir retreated to this

Massive oleander shrubs flank the entrance drive that leads toward the painter's house. The billowing multitude of color is underplanted with a ribbon of lavender cotton, Santolina Chamaecyparissus, *which mirrors the foliage of the towering olive trees behind.*

Overleaf: A late afternoon view across the downward grassy slope dotted with massive olive trees. Once typical of the French Côte d'Azur, it was this same vista that provoked Renoir to purchase the property in 1907.

simple life and compatible surroundings in which to continually work. Daily the artist would venture outside, paintbrushes strapped to his frail hands, to his world of olive trees, iris beds, or orderly rows of vegetables, to record the constant passages of time as reflected through light and changing form. If poor weather conditions forced the painter indoors, cuttings of roses or orange or olive branches were brought inside for Renoir to paint. This relationship with the garden was something the artist continued to pursue in his work.

Today the property, which is preserved as a museum with the house and studio open to the public, lies amid the highly populated coastline. It remains as Renoir's personal attempt to shelter and defend a small verdant remnant of the past for the future.

JOAQUIN SOROLLA

MADRID / SPAIN
1912

Opposite: The rectangular reflecting pool mirrors the leafy shadows of another corner of Joaquin Sorolla's garden, first planted in 1912 at the height of the artist's fame. The painter would often work outdoors capturing the effects of light and color in his patio garden. Numerous statues are set about the garden, many by the artist himself, and increase the feeling of space as they are discovered within the dense vegetation of acanthus, or boxwood and myrtle trees.

By the sixteenth century when the Moors were finally driven from the Iberian peninsula, they left behind the long tradition of incorporating water into both their garden and architectural spaces. The Alhambra and Granada are but two of the most famous examples that rely on the complex systems of hydraulics, which have become a standard in the Spanish garden vocabulary. The sonorous splashing of water jets and dripping fountains enlivens Sorolla's garden and echoes throughout the entire space.

Not long into the early years of this century, at a time when movements in art were producing radical changes of visual perception, this garden was conceived, the essence of a gentler past. Here, within the expanding urban setting of Madrid, the Spanish Impressionist painter Joaquin Sorolla composed a garden that reflected his native country's traditions and diverse cultural patrimony. This walled garden is inherently the mirrored image of a vitality permeated with pleasure and delight, a secluded place of diversion and a refuge of verdant contentment, which captures the innocent enjoyments of Sorolla's prolific life.

Joaquin Sorolla is an interesting phenomenon, although quite prevalent within the archives of art history. The painter's overwhelming success in his day was eventually eclipsed by the radical movements that coincided with his artistic productivity and only now, nearly one hundred years later, is his work re-acknowledged and appreciated again. Born in Valencia in 1863 and orphaned at the age of two, the painter studied in Spain before setting off for Italy and later Paris. By the turn of the century, the artist had been distinguished with the Grand Prix for painting at the 1900 Paris Exposition in competition with such fellow artists as John Singer Sargent, Sir Lawrence Alma-Tadema, and Gustav Klimt. As Sorolla's acclaim grew during the early years of the century, his artistic capacity increased to such heights that by 1906 he showed five hundred paintings in a commercial Parisian art gallery. Successfully recognized throughout Europe as well as South America and the United States, Sorolla was once known as Spain's greatest living painter.

In his work Sorolla attempted to depict the essence of his native homeland and its particular bright light. The exuberant Spanish life, with its traditions of festivals and processions, corridas and open-air markets, was caught as fleeting moments by Sorolla. His scenes of village life and seascapes were rendered in a direct, Impressionist manner with quick brushstrokes conjuring the simplicity of a relaxed yet complex cultural tradition. This heritage of united vocabularies was interpreted to create a garden of alluring and engaging beauty. Sorolla's Madrid garden is one of sensual delights, enabling the visitor to cast aside the outside world. The long tradition in Spain that goes back to the time of the Moors, has produced another counterpoint to the Northern European garden definition. The concept of the planted patio within the confines of a house was introduced into Spanish culture with the arrival of the Muslims in the eighth century. Courtyards and interior gardens were enchantingly transformed by the use of water: pools, rills, jets, and fountains create a sonorous effect, a captivating atmosphere of serenity. Sorolla, drawing from the history that has produced such gardens as the Alhambra and Granada, incorporated the concept of moving water into his small city plot, which seductively transformed the space. Two fountains linked by a long rill with splashing jets break against the multicolored ceramic tiles. In another area of his garden, screened behind a colonnade of statues and stone pillars shaded by wisteria, is a large rectangular-shaped reflecting pool, animated by the fountainhead above.

Pruned boxwood laid out in geometric lines reinforces the axial delineations and forms a succession of visual barriers that break up the garden into smaller intimate spaces. To enhance the effects of greater spatial dimension, strong verticals were placed by the artist to draw the eye upward. A shady pergola, freestanding columns, statues on plinths, and sycamore tree trunks all add to the visual impression of a larger garden space. The planting of shade-casting magnolias, sycamores, and pink-flowering acacia trees heightens the spatial sensations of moving from areas of full sun to cool dark shadows. Encircling the central fountain Sorolla planted myrtles from Granada, which still exist, as well as apple, plum, and cherry trees.

Within the shady folds a variety of rich foliage is bedded out with large-leafed acanthus, intermixed with irises and ferns. In the great Mediterranean tradition, and particularly characteristic of Spain, simple terra-cotta pots are set out everywhere. In full sun, potted

A detail of the tiled bench with incised heraldic stone carvings. The high-backed bench acts as a visual screen at the axial line terminus of the water rill.

pink and coral geraniums along with bush peppers, *Capsicum annuum,* with its tomatolike garnet fruits, line the water features and are tucked into the shadowy recesses. Climbing vines of twisting jasmine, wisteria, and the double-flowering yellow rose, *Rosa banksiae* 'Lutea', first introduced to the Iberian peninsula in the eighteenth century, scale the architectural columns and pergolas.

Joaquin Sorolla painted his garden, which he created in the heart of Madrid. Its intimate pleasures, verdant textures, and architectural detailing make this a place of retreat, which captivates us still.

Originally constructed in 1910 by Sorolla, the painter's house and adjoining studio, seen here, predate the garden by two years. Drawing from the rich Andalusian architectural vocabulary that was very much in vogue in the early decades of the twentieth century, Sorolla incorporated a central patio, fountains, freestanding columns, brightly colored ceramic tiles, and a vine-clad arcade into his Madrid garden. Set against the soft ocher-painted exterior walls are two terra-cotta pots planted with camellias, creating a distant focal point for one of the shaded axial pathways.

Behind the central fountain area, the shaded pergola is overplanted with yellow flowering Banksia roses intertwined with wisteria. Sorolla used ceramic tiles, concrete embedded with pebbles, and terra-cotta pavers to further enrich the garden. Here, bright blue-and-white curved edging tiles, border pathways, and defined planting beds increase the variety of visual experiences.

Overleaf: Viewed from the second story of Sorolla's Madrid studio, the central garden is composed of fountains and a water rill with jets that recall large-scale Islamic gardens. Employing plants and architectural elements characteristic of Spanish gardens, Sorolla imbued a feeling of intimacy among the three different areas of his patio garden, tucked neatly within the city center.

VANESSA BELL AND DUNCAN GRANT

CHARLESTON FARMHOUSE
EAST SUSSEX / ENGLAND
1919

Opposite: The tall, erect yellow spires of Ligularia ste-
nocephala *'The Rocket' and spent foxglove contrast
against the jagged toothed foliage and the blush roses
that creep up the brick and flint stone wall. The long
narrow bed that runs the exterior length of the garden
enclosure at Charleston is planted with semishade varieties, including aucubas, hellebores, hostas, montbretia,
and iris, which together form a mass of unchecked
growth and provides a succession of flowering periods.*

*A view across the cut flower garden from the farthest
point within the walled enclosure at Charleston. The
utilitarian plots were laid out in regimented rows of
flowers grown for the house intermixed with herbs and
vegetables, such as dahlias, penstemons, cornflowers,
and French beans and tomatoes.*

The Charleston Farmhouse and garden are dynamic affirmations of the great artistic accomplishments of its two principal creators, Vanessa Bell and her lifelong companion, Duncan Grant. Nestled in the grassy downs of southern England, the restored garden today characterizes the high-spirited individuality and creative talents of both artists. Deeply rooted in the English cottage-style tradition of the walled enclosure and uncontrived, common plantings, the East Sussex garden displays unorthodox uses of color, texture, and a wide range of construction materials employed. Combined with these elements are flourishes of whimsy and references to imported garden vocabularies, all of which reflect both artists' awareness and participation in the changing developments of modern art during the first half of the twentieth century. Equally illustrated in the garden is the personalized environment designed by Bell and Grant for their extended family and close-knit circle of friends. Like the enchanted farmhouse interiors, the garden at Charleston has a familiar, unassuming atmosphere. While neither grand nor overtly dramatic, both the house and garden portray the domestic world of a highly sophisticated and intellectual community.

Vanessa Bell and Duncan Grant first came to live at Charleston in the autumn of 1916, after Bell's sister and brother-in-law, Virginia and Leonard Woolf, found the isolated farmhouse for rent. Just miles inland from the English Channel and outside the town of Lewes in East Sussex, the complex of walled garden, orchard, and house had originally been built as tenant quarters for farmers working on the nearby Firle estate. Constructed in the local vernacular of brick and flintstone dating mostly from the late seventeenth and early eighteenth centuries, Charleston provided the required space for family and friends, plus being in close proximity to Vanessa Bell's sister, who then lived at nearby Asheham House. As an original member of the Bloomsbury group that included Vanessa's husband, Clive Bell; the Woolfs; Roger Fry, the art critic; Lytton Strachey, the biographer; as well as Duncan Grant, Vanessa Bell took on the house as a weekend country retreat. Freed from the conventions of London life, the members of the Bloomsbury group were able to live and work in the bohemian atmosphere that characterized Charleston. Although the farmhouse symbolized the protected and enclosed world existing within the tight confines of English society, both Bell and Grant and the other inhabitants were far from isolated. Both painters spent great amounts of time in London and traveled annually to the Continent, mixing with the European artistic community and with such artists as André Derain, Georges Braque, and Pablo Picasso.

By 1916, Duncan Grant and Vanessa Bell were widely exhibited painters in London and Paris as well as directors of Roger Fry's famous Omega Workshops, created in 1913. Employing young artists such as Wyndham Lewis and Gaudier-Brzeska, the cooperative workshop produced numerous textiles, furniture, and painted pottery, including those with designs by Fry, Bell, and Grant. Ceasing to exist by 1919, the Omega Workshop had a vast effect on the English decorative arts throughout the twentieth century. Both Bell and Grant continued after its demise to design rugs, tablewares, and textiles for leading British commercial companies well into the 1940s. The well-known painted interiors of Charleston Farmhouse remain the greatest example of their decorative painting work. Flowers, their garden, and surrounding landscape are all recurring themes employed by the artists in their decorative work as well as in their painted canvases, capturing the spirit and gaiety of bright color and natural forms.

It was not until after World War I that Vanessa Bell and Duncan Grant made significant transformations in the walled garden originally planted with fruit trees and vegetable rows. Straight, thin pathways of crushed stone were laid out, edged in brick and encircling the rectangular enclosed space. A narrow gravel terrace running the length of the house became an extension of the ground-floor rooms for good-weather seating. Toward one end of the terrace, a rectangular-shaped lawn was seeded, only one-eighth of the total garden, edged

Numerous sculptural pieces are set about at Charleston, including this nude protectively sur-
rounded by wavelike boxwood hedges that divide the garden in two. Placed as the focal point of
a long pathway, the marble statue is shaded by the canopy of an ancient apple tree. Many other
sculptures were homemade projects taken on by the family as events in which everyone
participated.

with a low santolina hedge and a brightly colored tile reflecting pool. Vegetables relegated beyond the walled garden to the outlying paddocks were replaced with large geometric-shaped beds and long borders. In 1933, a boxwood hedge replanted from outside the enclosure to the far end of the garden formed two half-hidden spaces behind. The ancient apple trees remained to provide verticals, thus increasing the sense of space. Flower beds along the perimeter walls and flanking the lawn were packed with bright, strongly colored annuals and perennials, which required the help of a full-time gardener, Mr. Stevens, to maintain. By 1945 Bell wrote that the paths had almost completely disappeared under the abundance of growth.

Color was also of great importance, as were the loud, vibrant associations of contrasting hues. The muted silver-leafed foliage of artemesia, *Achillea* 'The Pearl', and globe thistles were set against bold, yellow dashes of dinner-plate-size sunflowers or masses of varying reds; flowering tobacco, fuchsias, and deep-hued daylilies were enlivened with touches of yellow- or blue-tinged hostas. For the most part, the plantings at Charleston remained "old-fashioned" garden varieties found in cottage plots across the country such as peonies, poppies, asters, columbines, hollyhocks, and iris. A great many of the plants were repeated in other beds like roses, catmint, and yarrow, creating varying effects of mood or sensation. Plants were allowed to grow rampant and wild, some seeding themselves and engulfing pathways and neighboring beds. Roses such as *Rosa* 'Bobbie James' or *R.* 'Honorine de Brabrant' were trained up the existing apple trees and the surrounding flint stone walls. Sweet pea and espaliered *Choisya ternata* and pear trees were interplanted with the roses and clematis. An exception to the strong color theme was the use of pale or white flowers, such as *Clematis* montana, 'Iceberg' roses, or Easter lilies.

Both the garden and house at Charleston suggest a relaxed simplicity and humble refinement. Punctuating the garden at irregular intervals are statues and pots, benches and reflecting pools made of such materials as plaster or piled brick, which all have a wonderful handmade feel and sense of innocence. Further personalizing the garden are plaster busts, sculpted by Duncan Grant, that line the garden walls. The "piazza" area of the garden, set behind the undulating boxwood hedge, was made in 1946 and was one of the last major elements added to the garden. The hard surface area for seating is composed of near-perfect alignments of brick and broken crockery (some pieces designed originally by Bell and Grant), which imply joyful afternoons spent in its creation. The pleasure contained within the garden walls is a measure of Vanessa Bell and Duncan Grant's artistic accomplishments.

Today, the garden and farmhouse are owned and maintained by the Charleston Trust and in 1984 under the direction of Sir Peter Shepheard the garden was restored with funding from Lila Acheson Wallace, who was also greatly responsible for the restoration of Claude Monet's Giverny. Both Vanessa Bell and Duncan Grant's painted works, collections of photographs, journals, and letters were consulted in addition to recollections of living family and friends, when restoring the garden. Open to the public since 1986, the garden has returned to its former glory as a place of unassuming beauty and distinct personality.

A vignette composed of a statue fragment and assorted collection of potted annuals—nasturtiums and pansies, with geraniums and begonias.

Pages 60–61: Helichrysum angustifolium, *top-heavy and blown down after a summer shower, unfurls itself and adds to the casual air of the cottage-style informality that is so evocative of Charleston. Composed of geometrically shaped planting beds, with pathways laid out on axis to various rooms of the house, the strong lines of the gardens are completely obscured by midsummer in an overabundance of foliage, such as penstemons, anthemis, hardy geraniums, and dead-nettles.*

Pages 62–63: The billowing beds of varying heights, contrasting textures, and rich colors are characteristic of the unique quality that Vanessa Bell produced when she went about planning the garden at Charleston Farmhouse. The luxuriousness of full blown, surging masses of perennials, shrubs, trees, and climbing vines are embellished with flourishes of whimsy, which sets this garden apart from so many. The bold dot of the golden sunflower popping from the clouds of globe thistles and poppies, or the pristine white Easter lilies engulfed within the wide drifts of sedum, pale yellow Anthemis *and mallows, reflect the artist's personal vision of a bold joyfulness and pleasure in life.*

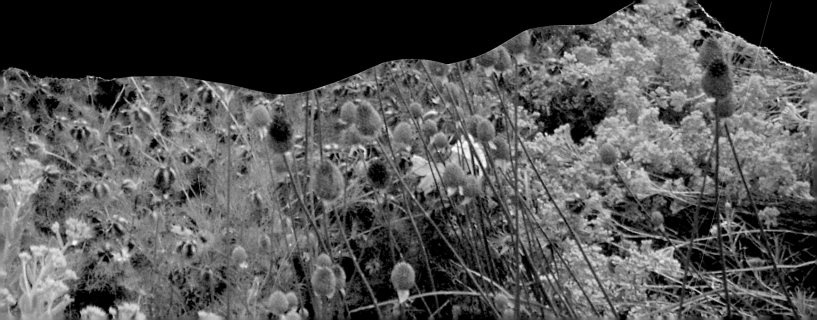

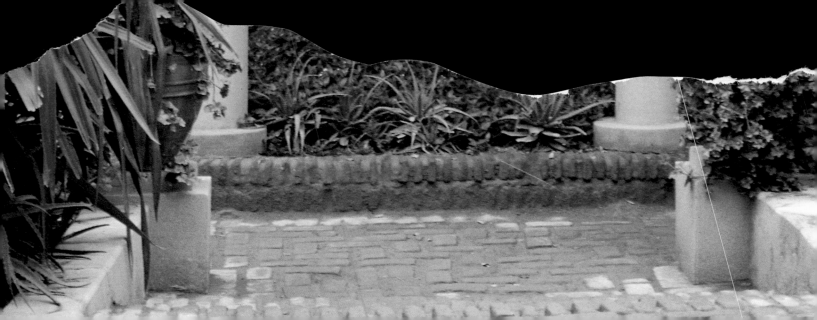

JACQUES MAJORELLE

MARRAKECH / MOROCCO
1933

Opposite: A giant bower of flowering bougainvillea is supported by rose-colored columns at the intersection of two pathways. A constant variety of changing levels and directional possibilities increases the sensation of walking through this jungled labyrinth. Although Majorelle often painted in the garden, the verdant imagery usually became a backdrop for his figurative subjects.

Jacques Majorelle repainted his studio a cobalt blue and yellow in 1933 as well as the stair railings, fountain features, and terra-cotta pots, such as this one planted with purple heart, Setcreasea pallida. *The shades of brilliant blues, pinks, and yellows precede the monochromatic interventions by the Mexican architect Luis Barragán or the Brazilian landscape architect and painter Roberto Burle Marx.*

The giant palms sway in the sand-filled breezes and dusk appears on the horizon. In the fading twilight, the garden takes on an entirely new character as the dense shadows become deeper and the cobalt blue constructions turn pitch-black. The inky water surfaces throughout the garden mirror the varying degrees of still darkness that veil the garden.

Majorelle's is one of the century's most extraordinary garden experiences. The relatively modest scale is deceiving and the atmosphere of enchanting intimacy wholly engulfing. Its importance does not lie entirely in a radical layout nor in unequaled plant diversity, although the garden far surpasses most, but rather in the unparalleled design approach as the act of a singular creation. For most artists, the act of painting results from a process based on direct observation and imagination. This quest empowers an artist with the unique ability to reshape given objects and to reform standard norms. In some instances, however, an artist's secondary obsession comes to overshadow his principal work. This is true of Jacques Majorelle, an artist whose unending desire to paint prepared him to create one of the most beautifully moving and passionate of gardens.

For nearly forty years until his death in 1962, Jacques Majorelle came to know well the continent of Africa. Born in 1886 the only child of Louis Majorelle, the celebrated furniture-maker of the Art Nouveau School of Nancy, the artist studied architecture before devoting himself to painting. After brief periods attending Parisian art academies, Majorelle traveled to Spain, Italy, Greece, and Egypt, where he spent four years. Ill health exempted him from military service and prompted the suggestion to visit Morocco. Finally taking up residence in 1917 at the base of the Atlas Mountain chain in the pink-hued city of Marrakech, Majorelle

Reflected against the murky depths of the huge fish tank, the dappled specks of sunlight animate the water's surface. The Majorelle garden has been meticulously and beautifully restored by Pierre Bergé and Yves Saint Laurent. Open to the public, the garden intoxicates the visitor with its mysterious atmosphere of junglelike vegetation.

was eventually to create a complex garden composition that captured his appreciation for this adopted culture. Situated on the edge of the sand-swept palm grove forest, Majorelle built a Moroccan-inspired pavilion villa and adjoining studio.

Off a bustling major thoroughfare lies a dirt road lined with massive pink and white oleanders, which leads to a blue-tiled portal and green-painted door. A high wall of compact earth encircles and protects the garden within. Past the entrance there is a moment of hesitation, for it is dark and the trail is in shadow. A raised red-colored concrete path seems to cut through a dense grove of bamboo. The harsh, hot light of the exterior is filtered as the dappled sunlight patterns animate the bare earth floor.

It is cool and both the sound and tactile sensation of water fill the air. There is a feeling of extreme luxuriance and privilege as one walks into this exotic world. The garden is made up of familiar, if not basic, regional elements that the painter experienced on his journeys into the Moroccan culture and traditions. The singular character of the garden results from the way in which he reassembled the varying units to create an original work. Within less than an acre of land, Majorelle formed this tranquil, vaguely mysterious world.

Raised walks, on the average a foot high or so, are punctuated with constant changes in elevation, which rise or descend by means of brick or tile steps. Secondary pathways and narrow trails lead off in straight directions and turn abruptly or curve in or bow out around masses of vegetation. This labyrinth of perplexing walkways is deceiving. Crossing darkened corners or opening onto sun-drenched patches, the garden scale increases at each curious step. The sense of secrecy and enigma also makes the visitor even more aware of the often forbidding vegetation that billows and spills out onto the garden circuit.

During his numerous travels to paint as far south as the Ivory Coast or up into the higher reaches of the Atlas chain, Majorelle would return with specimens he had collected. Over the years exchanges were made with botanical gardens abroad along with other collectors, making for a garden rich in diverse exotic varieties. In 1933, two years after he built the Robert Mallet Stevens–inspired cube-shaped painting studio which was void of any exterior decoration, the garden was transformed with the use of applied color as never witnessed before. Incorporating strong vivid hues and earthy tones, Majorelle employed them on a scale far larger than any preceding garden example. The deep red of the rampart walls and sun-dried clay was used for the walkways and various garden gazebos. The studio building was painted in a brilliant cobalt blue and trimmed in an intense accent of chrome yellow, as were the unadorned fountains, water rills, garden pots, large fish tank, and viewing platform.

The overpowering abundance of succulents, cacti, palms, and flowering vines is intoxicating. Jade trees, euphorbias, and echeverias are intermixed with melon-shaped pincushion cactus, and rising from spiked beds of agaves and aloes are twisted stocks of totem pole cacti, which all reconfirm the surrealism of the place. Banana tree fronds, *Cycas revoluta*, caladiums, and palmetto mounds nearly enshroud pathways, creating vegetal mazelike walls. Soaring palm tree trunks provide robust verticals which draw the vision toward the fertile blue sky. The higher reaches of the treetops of dragon trees, *Dracaena draco*, the fan fonds of the Fiji Island palm, *Pritchardia pacifica*, and the bowers of bamboos are heavily weighed and arch over with the tangled masses of purple and magenta bougainvillea gone wild.

At times the light is blindingly bright and the sky intensely blue. When the sun hits the cobalt-colored architecture, it transforms it to almost black in color, which merges in turn with the heavy-cast shadows of the leafy vegetation. At that moment—which can last an entire day—in the deep recessed folds and under the multitude of foliage layers, the variety of gray-green and variegated masses becomes ethereal and creates an underwater effect in the garden.

Water, a primary element in all Islamic gardens and of vital importance in the hot, dry climate of Marrakech, was integrated throughout the garden, thus creating the intensely lush and flourishing environment. An elaborate system of canals passes under the raised walks and floods each planted area, also infusing the air with tiny dewdrops. The faint, distant splashing sounds echo from the water rills, fountain jets, and jumping frogs and fish that inhabit the large tank, adding to the trancelike effect.

Late afternoon is the time of day when the light changes dramatically, shifting into that famous Marrakech color, pink. At this moment the garden is transformed into its noctural counterpart. The brash violent reds, deep purples, and magentas begin to recede. The pale yellow water lilies emerge and the forbidding, pastel-colored flowers of the fatal datura begin to glow. Equally mysterious and unsettling, the garden takes on its variety of different nighttime nuances, and one begins to wonder if this isn't heaven on earth.

Overlooking the square reflecting pool and fountain, the attached wooden porch of Majorelle's painting studio was one of the many decorative additions carried out in 1933. Also at that time, the artist transformed the garden with the introduction of bright, vivid color. The illusion of vast space is projected by the dense plantings and mazelike system of raised pathways.

Pages 70–71: Shaded by the towering groves of pritchardias and banana trees, the cobalt blue-painted pergola is blanketed in wisteria and bougainvillea vines. The garden projects a riotous sensation of teeming growth sporadically unchecked. In reality, eight gardeners maintain the verdant jungle, constantly pruning, replanting, watering, and sweeping the red-colored walks. Clusters of nympheas grown in the water tank require an annual pruning to keep their invasive vegetation in check.

Pages 72–73: In Majorelle's day, the cactus and succulent beds that surround the square fountain were of enormous size and height with interwoven agaves, aloes, and cacti creating a surrealistic mixed border. Replanted during restoration, with time the bed will return to its former state. The long water canal disappears into the dark recesses of vegetation and adds to the garden's implied greater size.

HENRY MOORE

HOGLANDS
HERTFORDSHIRE / ENGLAND
1940

Opposite: A towering pair of oaks, Quercus robur 'fastigiata', *are overrun with climbing ivy and form a ghostly silhouette against the open meadow beyond. The simplicity of such landscape elements is juxtaposed with a wide variety of the sculptor's large-scale works.*

The overrun state of Hoglands has produced a number of phantasmagorical shapes that dot the property and imbue it with an air of drama, such as this variegated ivy, Hedera sp., *that has entirely engulfed a small fruit tree.*

Henry Moore's Hoglands compound is a bewildering place, a place possessed by a dramatic force. Unaffected by grandiose gestures and unassuming in plant varieties chosen, the property projects a particular grandeur in the most informal way. The land is fairly flat, the sky open and far-reaching, and vegetation, while maintained and tended to, has an almost unruly character. It is a gardenscape of defined areas, of simple enclosures and natural horizons juxtaposed in a broad-sweeping and expressive manner. The composing elements at Hoglands of sky, trees, meadows, and mowed grass are interactive and startling in their scale. The landscape has undeniably altered since the death of the sculptor in 1986 and his wife, Irina Moore, in 1989, yet it still retains a dynamic quality that provokes an emotional response to the numerous massive sculptural works by the artist that dot the property.

Prior to World War II, and for the years since their marriage in 1929, the Moores participated in the artistic and intellectual community that eventually converged in Hampstead, which included Barbara Hepworth, the sculptor, her husband, Ben Nicolson, the painter, and for briefer periods, Piet Mondrian and Sigmund Freud. With the approaching war and fear of bombings, many members of the Hampstead group fled London for the safer countryside. The Moores were finally forced to do the same in 1940, after a bomb fell near their studio during the Blitz, blowing out doors and windows. Moving north of the city to the county of Hertfordshire, they settled in the hamlet of Perry Green, where they found a share in a seventeenth-century farmhouse. With the proceeds of a sculpture made by Moore, the couple made a down payment on the house.

Set in low, undulating wheat fields and sheep meadows, the one-acre farmstead at Hoglands increased in size to nearly a 70-acre complex over the next forty years. As Henry Moore became more successful, the Moores were able to buy additional lands, annexing neighboring woods, pastures, and farms. Irina Moore was greatly responsible for working with the planting of the grounds and developing the various planted beds. Her unassuming style and treatment of the perennial borders and foundation beds surrounding the house were characterized by simple, commonly found plants and flowers. Even today, Irina Moore's grander landscape work can still be observed throughout the estate.

Moving beyond the house, the visitor experiences the subtle changes in the landscape. The focal attention is drawn outward by the creation of a series of informal enclosures and obstacles that force the viewer to continue onward. As the terrain begins to open up, the scale too becomes vast. Thick privet hedges delineate certain areas while low, two-foot-high hawthorn hedges meander at points, encircling a sculpture and disappearing within a tangled mass of vegetation beyond. The eye is always wandering, discovering glimpses of Moore's glimmering white marble or streaked bronze sculptures half-hidden in the folds of trees and shrubs.

Farther out, the landscape is scattered with varying shaped studio structures and sculptural pieces displayed in well-organized green frames and placed against individualized plant groups or open sky. The parklike setting allows the visitor to move easily among the sculptures. The absence of formal, delineated enclosures or compartmentalized surrounds increases the simplicity of the place. Large, tightly packed arrangements of boxwood, lilac bushes, or dwarf conifers, as well as silver-leafed maple, purple beech, blue Atlas cedar, and birch trees planted within irregular, kidney-shaped beds, aid in the continual movement of the eye. Creating screens or backdrops for the artist's work, strategically placed willows punctuate the open mowed areas.

By 1977, when the artist established the Henry Moore Foundation and deeded works of art and land to the foundation—excepting his home, Hoglands—the estate consisted of nine different working studios, cottages for assistants, storage units, barns, greenhouses, and Quonset huts. Hoglands now remains under the care of the couple's daughter, Mary Moore, who is restoring the garden features nearest the house to their former glory.

Many of the works on the grounds of the Henry Moore Foundation date to the artist's later years, such as the sculptor's Sheep Piece *of 1971–72. Moore placed the large sculpture within the Hertfordshire pastureland.*

Pages 78–79: The dark twisted trunks and gnarled branches of an English hawthorn, Crataegus laevigata, *grove delineate the property line between the Henry Moore Foundation lands and the artist's private residence, now under restoration. The tree row, or the irregularly spaced apple trees that dot the property, add drama to the parklike setting.*

Pages 80–81: Beneath the skeleton of an old fruit tree a wave of variegated yellows and greens enliven a border near Moore's house. A columnar cypress, Chamaecyparis lawsoniana columaris glauca, *rises from the spreading tendrils of a yellow-tipped juniper, and the clouds of* Achemilla mollis *and* Lamium.

ALPHONSO OSSORIO

THE CREEKS
EAST HAMPTON / LONG ISLAND / NEW YORK
1952

Opposite: The explosion of color that delighted Ossorio was produced in a number of ways. Here, a Japanese Red maple is electrified by the cool green fronds of the Royal fern Osmunda regalis *growing through the lacy carmine leaves. The artist would also graft together many different cultivars to create imagery completely foreign to nature.*

One of the few remaining features from the estate's former layout is the wide spreading yew that is supported by brightly painted red and blue poles that carry the weight of the 100-year-old tree. All the conifers, still carefully pruned and shaped to enhance their individual characters, are overseen by the artist's inheritor, Ted Dragon, who lived with Ossorio at The Creeks since 1952. One of the only formally laid-out straight walks in the garden, the colorful vertical becomes a visual focal point for the allée planted with varieties of blue-tinged cedars and creeping junipers.

When rare compositions of a strongly personal vision occur, they can at first appear startling, if not bizarre. Monet's Giverny or Gertrude Jekyll's Munstead Wood were certainly novel gardens in their day, yet they have come to exercise a lasting and singularly strong influence on our sense of composition and design. Such a place unknown yet within the possibilities of influence is the unique gardenscape created by the late artist Alphonso Ossorio. From the early 1960s until his death in 1990, Ossorio forged a vast garden complex where he played on variations of a single theme. There on the far eastern shores of New York's Long Island, the artist expressed his particular spirited vision of paradise. Whereas many gardens often reflect the passions of an era, tradition, or style, Ossorio's unique landscape is an example of the passions of his great mind.

Born in the Philippines in 1916 to a wealthy family, the artist was sent to school in England before coming to America to attend Harvard University in Cambridge, Massachusetts. At the outbreak of World War II, Ossorio (by then a naturalized citizen) was enlisted in the United States Army as a military illustrator. His finely detailed, almost grotesque drawings of wounded soldiers made on the battlefields evoke a strong affinity for the surreal, which resurfaced in his later paintings, sculptures, and most strikingly in his garden. The Creeks undoubtedly was to become Ossorio's finest artistic creation, or congregation, as he called his three-dimensional sculptures.

Ossorio purchased the large estate in 1952 after learning of its sale from the painters Jackson Pollock and Lee Krasner. Built in 1889 on the shore of the saltwater Georgica Pond in Easthampton, the Mediterranean-style house overlooks the marshes eastward to the Atlantic Ocean. Home originally to the fashionable painters Albert and Adele Herter, it was the artistic center for the summer residential community during the turn of the century. In its day, thirty Japanese gardeners tended the large gardens that included radiating formal borders, vast rose beds, and a square acre consisting entirely of blue irises. An air of exoticism prevailed with gondola embankments, theatricals, grapevine porticos, and various water gardens. Ossorio added land to his initial purchase to form 57 acres and he dramatically altered the entire estate while retaining its particular atmosphere of exotic unfamiliarity.

A sense of forbidding pleasures begins at the property entrance. A pair of vividly painted red, white, and blue posts mark the gate; just beyond, shadows from nearby pine trees obscure the drive as it turns and fades into the vista. At first glance, the road seems to cross a mysterious forest dotted with curious shapes in bright yellows, vivid greens, and blues. It is only after a few moments that one realizes with amazement that the vistas that open up or crowd in and engulf the drive are composed entirely of a variety of conifers. The landscape is eerie, if not weirdly bizarre. The glaucous-tinged cedars, junipers, and cypress are set against variegated tipped pines, spruce, and firs. Ossorio strove to make dramatic contrasts of evergreen groups and enliven the already heady mix with massive sculptural pieces of his own construction. Composed of an odd assembly of found objects and painted in alternating yellows, reds, whites, blacks, and blues, the pure pigments increase the spatial tension and draw the eye toward particular conifer compositions. Conventional landscape practices of juxaposing foliages or contrasting hues are vastly exaggerated here for Ossorio mixed three, four, and at times five or six different colors together in a single massive group. To intensify the red of a Japanese maple, Ossorio planted it against vivid green ferns or golden-tinged cypress. His combinations never subtle nor intended to be, were rather wildly gone mad.

To increase the sense of an unreal world, the artist planted conifers of every contorted variety closer to walks and the drive. Twisted trunks, weeping branches, fastigiate trees, and prostrate creepers add to the atmosphere of a supernatural world. Color is used to add an element of vibrancy and dramatic form, yet in this dazzling environment another sensation takes hold. After amazement and shock subside, a peculiar sense of peace occurs. The sea breezes filter the light cast from the garden's blues, yellows, and greens, bathing the property

The garden view that recedes toward the marshes of Georgica Pond is enlivened with various plantings of Lawson cypress cultivars, junipers, blue Atlas cedars, and the artist's own sculptures. Ossorio's work is composed of found objects, such as these painted ocean buoys set at opposing heights in relation to the diminishing perspective. This play on perceived spatial distance increases the surreal atmosphere of the landscape.

in an almost aquatic atmosphere. The absence of formal walks and pathways forces visitors to discover the landscape for themselves. This lack of direction actually allows one to experience the seamless flow of the garden.

Ossorio's passion began as a means to create a year-round garden. For nearly thirty years it was his total obsession. When collecting specimens, he never thought twice about purchasing a rare conifer, whether available nearby or from somewhere across the world. His collection is one of the most extraordinary of its kind and rivals those in the world's largest botanical gardens. Ossorio's gardenscape, so curious, so weird, and so delightfully unique, is also powerfully moving and filled with life. Intense blocks of color and phantasmagorical shapes are formed to create an intensely personal expression. It is a garden to be experienced from within and one waiting to be discovered by the outside world. As the two-mile drive returns to the highway and passes a second set of painted portals, one stops to close the gate, and turns back to see if it was actually a reality and not just a wild dream.

The vitality and energy that radiate from the landscape can be overpowering. The nonconventional groupings of conifers selected for their opposing colors and distorted forms were one of Ossorio's greatest achievements. Although not following common trends, nor likely to launch a major movement, the dramatic action the artist created within the space is interesting and applicable. The all-evergreen garden relies on the ever-changing effects of light and shadow to form seasonal alterations. The clarity of the small-leafed azalea, blue spruce, Hinoki cypress, and pine tree plantings, seen here on a misty summer morning, change dramatically in the cooler light of winter.

The contrasting color associations that Ossorio so attentively worked for makes for a garden rich in visual surprises. Every hardy example north of the 40th parallel is represented in the garden—contorted, weeping, fastigiate, and prostrate, as well as normal forms. Here the bright red-painted swimming pool surround heightens the visual brilliance of the blues, golden yellows, and greens.

Overleaf: Like players on a stage, Ossorio constantly uprooted and moved the various conifers until he was completely satisfied with their spatial relationships to one another. Here in the Owl Garden, the changing canvas of colors and textural form alters at every step, increasing the sensation of being part of a foreign alien world. Of the few deciduous trees on the property, Ossorio used contorted witch-hazels and copper beeches for their unusual purple-tinged foliage. Oddly enough, this madness of spirit makes for a certain tranquility and peace when experienced from within the garden.

ISAMU NOGUCHI

MURE
THE ISLAND OF SHIKOKU / JAPAN
1955

Opposite: One of the earliest Japanese garden concepts dating back to the fifteenth century is that of the dry landscape garden technique. The physical presence of stones, and their particular arrangement, is intended to provoke a sense of movement and to further bind the viewer to the actual setting. In 1984, Noguchi created the evocation of a tumbling downstream movement, thus re-creating the speed, sound, and energy of rushing water. The flowering shrub adds a single note of color and focuses the viewer's attention on the dry cascade flanked by dwarf bamboo. In the summer, the grassy slope is covered in wildflowers planted by the sculptor.

Against a backdrop of dense black pines and stone wall, a flowering ornamental cherry tree bursts forth with spring blossoms. The only one of its kind planted by the artist in the workshop confines, the cherry—like the magnolia or willows planted elsewhere in the garden— was intended to symbolize masses of cherry trees.

Often in an artist's work there exists the strong suggestion of a quest, a soul-searching of sorts. The dilemmas of the world, the preoccupations of a culture, or the particulars of a moment are projected into a self-contained expression. The final result of an artist's journey can produce profound influences on society and how we perceive ourselves and our surrounding world. Within the course of twentieth-century art, former standards of representation have been broadened and a creation, an artistic one, manifests itself in a multitude of shapes and forms. Isamu Noguchi was such an artist whose voyage was one of defining, and therefore attempting to understand, many of those universal truths common to us all. For a man whose great fame was worldwide and artistic productivity vast, Noguchi continued to press on, going deeper in his search for universal meaning. In the wake of his work, we are confronted with his redefinitions that draw a new beauty from our own environment. The landscape that Isamu Noguchi created on the Japanese island of Shikoku, amid piles of coarse rock and collected stone, is a garden that speaks a universal language that is perhaps hard to distinguish at first, until one realizes the vocabulary is very well known.

Isamu Noguchi was an interesting and complex man, with a past of diverging cultures and deep exposure to others. Japanese by parentage and American by birth and citizenship, during his lifetime the sculptor occupied the spatial distance between the two worlds which he tried to bridge through his work. He was born in California in 1904, spent his youth in Japan, and later studied in Paris under the tutelage of the sculptor Constantin Brancusi. Noguchi traveled extensively—to eastern Asia, India, Europe, and South America, which became his various artistic roots, along with trips to his two polar spiritual homelands, the United States and Japan. An artist of varied expression and great energy, he produced designs for the theater and ballet, and he designed furniture and what have come to be known as his famous paper lamps. A creator of numerous public gardens and vaster urban parks, Noguchi brought to his various endeavors a spiritual simplicity in an effort to capture a perfect intellectual harmony.

Rather late in his celebrated career, Noguchi first came to visit Shikoku on the southern reaches of the Inland Sea. Traveling in the mid-1950s in search of the perfect stone required for his Unesco sculpture piece, Noguchi came across the small stonecutter's village of Mure. Nestled against the rising granite cliffs of the surrounding mountains of Yakuri and Yashima with the sea nearby, it was here that the artist decided to create an eastern counterpart to his established New York complex of workshops, exhibition spaces, and gardens.

Believing stone to be the direct link to the center of meaning, Noguchi made it the primary material for his artistic works. Handpicked by the sculptor, examples came from across the continents: from far-off India or Sweden and the neighboring island of Yashima. The various stones are used to form a facile and unusual complex. Their presence in a variety of states created an extraordinary and personal kind of innovative landscape. Edging the approach to his property stones are discarded in every form, and cast-off shards and ground-up pebbles litter the country road. Within the walled compound, rock piles form the rough topography. Noguchi has said that he drew strength from the noble stones and that they in turn gave him a sense of inner peace. Mure is a fascinating place, though initially unsettling because it is so unfamiliar to Westerners. Void of the traditional elements that compose a gardenscape, the assorted collection of mismatched stones seems alive and nonetheless conveys the essences of a true garden landscape. In creating this modernist approach toward landscape, the artist used a number of age-old techniques based on the ancient tradition of Japanese temple and villa gardens. Seven-foot-tall dry-set stone walls were raised to develop a series of enclosures which define and give character to each space. Recalling the steep embankments of ancient fortified Japanese castles, the monumental boundaries are majestic and also protect the garden.

The artist's studio is situated in an open, light-filled space, a deliberate contrast to the heavily planted areas around Noguchi's residence. The workshop courtyards open up and are planted with single varieties of trees. The whitewashed work studio was an old kura, or storage barn, that Noguchi transported to the site piece by piece.

From the interior of the island Noguchi transported a two-hundred-year-old Samurai house to be his residence, painstakingly rebuilding the facade and otherwise modernizing it. Large sliding panels open onto a succession of vistas that recede toward the distant mountain view. Noguchi's borrowed landscape is framed by dense rows of black pine, which also screen the house from the workshop areas and envelop the residence in an atmosphere of mysterious shadow. Horse chestnut and beech trees were interplanted with groves of oak, maple, ash, and alders that create a forestlike backdrop to the sloped bank that rises behind the property. Void of low plantings such as shrubbery beds or borders, the enclosed walled courtyard spaces are treated with compacted earth and a sandy ground cover and are defined individually by billowing groups of willows or alianthus and single specimens silhouetted against the architectural elements. It is these single plantings that define this naturalistic, Japanese landscape.

The artist's treatment of space—or the absence thereof—is related directly to the concepts that governed ancient Japanese temple gardens. Their minimalist compositions describe a world where the mind is set free. Noguchi transposed these spiritual sensations of tranquility and peace into the contemporary context of Mure. As his final creation of a large-scale environment, Noguchi's visionary-like power produced a landscape of incredible beauty and presence. By converging centuries-old structures and unspoiled mountain views with trees, wildflower slopes, and stones, the artist unified the whole to reveal the timeless qualities of a place. His quest for a clear understanding of our world has produced a personal and extraordinary universe that will influence and challenge our definition of a garden.

A small garden area composed of bamboo and moss grows behind the artist's 200-year-old house. Massive stone walls and double rows of black pine create the sense of shade and seclusion, which balances the more spacious areas of the overall complex.

Opposite: In 1983 Noguchi undertook massive earthworks: he carved a series of informal terraced plateaus from the adjacent hillside. The large boulder path climbs the manmade slope, in which the sculptor used a variety of stone materials to evoke a succession of altering sensations. The crushed gravel, oversized stones, and thick slab steps reflect the Japanese tradition of imbuing a space with individual atmospheres. Thickets of bamboo line the walk and a strip of moss cushions one edge. Noguchi believed that asymmetrical composition made for a far richer garden environment.

Like the framed views from a temple platform, the sliding wall panels of the sculptor's studio open to reveal the sand court. Noguchi would place both finished and unfinished pieces here to be viewed in the round against the borrowed landscape of the distant mountains. The relation between the interior and exterior, the positive and negative, or light and shadow, were concepts of vital importance to the artist and his work. Noguchi incorporated the Japanese philosophical tradition of the Ma, which relates to the space between both positive and negative forces. The sculptor believed that the fact of enclosure, not just the bare space within, was equally important and that it had the power to project its own unique character.

Atop the second-highest plateau of Mure's manmade hill, Noguchi created a stone viewing platform. Entirely hidden from sight of the compound below, the platform is oriented toward views down the valley and out to the sea and islands in the distance. A place for retreat and contemplation, Noguchi's garden feature recalls temple viewing platforms and examples found in villa gardens such as Katsura in Kyoto.

Pages 98–99: Hewn stone shards and cast-off chips were always kept by Noguchi after a sculpture was completed and incorporated into the garden landscape. Noguchi believed that each stone and its fragments had a life and soul. Within the various enclosed courtyards finished works were placed on pedestals, which allowed viewing from all sides, something Noguchi felt was essential for his works to be properly understood.

Pages 100–101: The entrance to Isamu Noguchi's compound is marked by large groups of massive boulders and rough stone. Beyond the mammoth dry-set stone wall and tiled roofline of the artist's studio rise the craggy granite cliffs of the Yashima and Yakuri mountains. Noguchi incorporated many Japanese garden traditions into his site, including the concept of the "borrowed landscape." Here the strong vertical stones frame the distant view and establish the spirit of the place.

IAN HAMILTON FINLAY

LITTLE SPARTA
DUNSYRE / SCOTLAND
1966

Opposite: The artist makes repeated cross-references to the imagery and sensations of the seventeenth-century French painters who inspired the pastoral landscape movement, in this case with the poem engraved on the stone paver bedded in the grass here.

Reminiscent of Finlay's 1982 "Sacred Grove" installation at the Sculpture Park of the Kroller-Müller Museum in Holland, a sloped grassy bank of the higher garden is wooded and known as the Hillside Pantheon. Dedicated to the various poets, philosophers, and painters associated in spirit with the French Revolution, the artist has placed stone column footings at the base of trees. Mowed pathways connect the trees and with time the trunks will resemble columnar shafts. In the long tradition of celebrated odes within a landscape, Finlay, for example, evokes the Temple of British Worthies at Stowe in a totally contemporary context.

Outside the village of Dunsyre, a lonely road meanders along the billowing slopes of the Scottish Lowlands and at a certain point beyond an ancient stone bridge there appears a gravel drive clearly marked Stonypath. Turning to traverse pasturelands dotted with flocks of sheep and lazy, grazing cows, the rugged lane crosses a series of paddock gates before rising to the crest of a hill. In the distance of the next incline looms a verdant inhabited island. Like a lighthouse overlooking a foggy sea, Ian Hamilton Finlay's Little Sparta looms, a garden of visionary strength, wedged between the barren moors of the southern Pentlands Hills. It is at this site where the Scottish artist and poet has created a radically innovative landscape. A place where a garden wages war with the inequalities of society, Little Sparta displays inventive new concepts about landscape approach and design. Finlay's garden, both in its plantings and in the many inscriptions scattered throughout the property, evokes a classical "language" as a way of addressing contemporary issues.

Little Sparta is one of the most emotional and evocatively powerful garden experiences I know. Like Merlin, Finlay has magically transformed an abandoned shepherd's cottage and a lone ash tree into a penetrating maze of lucid sensations and audible atmospheres. In this austere landscape that has but a few months of climate suitable for cultivation, the artist has labored endlessly since 1966 when he moved his family to the property then known as Stonypath. Employing the materials at hand, be it either chiseled stone or mountain ash, raspberry bushes or brick and cobbled pavers, the artist has created a place of perpetual motion. This space provokes endless physical and intellectual responses as one is guided through the dense growth. The feeling of veiled layers appears as one walks at a slowed pace, uncovering half-hidden secrets. Finlay's garden is a laboratory of sorts and the primary setting for many of his works that once perfected are sent out and installed worldwide. At times the garden can be intimidating, as one is required not only to observe but to reflect on the crosscurrents of references from antiquity to the present day. Allusion is made repeatedly to the artist's pantheon of intellectual imagery, from Claude Lorrain and Poussin, to Rousseau, Corot, and the French revolutionary Saint-Just, along with contemporary quotations of modern warfare.

This is a sensitive place composed of a multitude of experiences that touch deep sentiments. Finlay's sculptural works are set within his conceived landscape. Some of them invoke anger or grief at the injustice of bloody hostilities or convey sensuous pleasures, such as the discovery of a pair of frolicking lovers which alludes to Bernini's Apollo and Daphne. Wind is a strong element in Finlay's landscape, which he uses to enhance the numerous nautical references set about the garden, reflecting his great passion for the rigged vessels that ply the Scottish coasts. Water trickling down a hillside, rerouted and renamed Virgil's Spring, becomes a gurgling brook planted with flag iris and large-leafed rhubarb or a placid mirror which reflects the silver-tinged alder groves. One of Finlay's earliest designs is the Roman garden, defined by arborvitae and pine trees, potted hostas, and statuary of World War II battleships as references to imperial power. In an ode to the memory of the German painter Caspar David Friedrich, Finlay has built a large stone pyramid within an enclosure of dark, forbiddingly romantic fir trees, which transport one beyond the Scottish moors. The beauty of Little Sparta and the simplified varieties of the plantings are matched by the precise symmetry and proportion of the garden elements. Cedar posts, wooden gates, brick piers, stone plaques, and sundials all portray an exact perfect detailing. A gentleness prevails within the garden, touched with whimsy and endless variations of plant materials which create a feeling of familiarity and make this a peaceful retreat.

From the moment one passes the garden's main gate with an inscribed portal that reads "a cottage a field a plough," to the time of departure when one deciphers "There is happiness," one has become marked with a unique experience that, like a lyrical note, will return to be played over and over again in one's memory.

The inscribed stone plaque set at the waters' edge of the mowed grass path that meanders around the Upper Pond is one of the numerous sculptural works by Finlay that the visitor happens upon at Little Sparta. These pure and seemingly simplistic interventions are in fact powerful devices that provoke strong emotional responses in relation to the landscaped garden and the surrounding natural environment. The harmony that exists between the uncomplicated plants employed by Finlay, such as the white rose of Scotland, the yellow raspberries, or the clumps of large-leafed rhubarb, and the classical references form a most unique and poetic garden experience.

A series of winding pathways meanders through the woodland garden at Little Sparta. Composed of secret areas dedicated to various monuments, people, or events, the artist's invented landscape contains such compositions as Julie's Garden, dedicated to classical lovers, the Grotto of Aeneas and Dido, the Pompeiian Garden, and the Allotment (Epicurean) Garden, where Finlay grows vegetables and herbs in strawberry beds. Transforming the barren moorland with wild cherries, sycamores, alders, fir trees, and Lawson cypress, the artist created the feeling of a classical pastoral landscape. Like starting off on a treasure hunt, the visitor is equipped with a detailed plan and proceeds to discover the concealed references set within Finlay's garden.

One of the first areas of Little Sparta to be treated by the artist was the Sunken Garden. The diamond-shaped pavers are marked with the names of Scottish boats that have caught the artist's imagination since childhood. Flanked on either side by borders of foxglove, Rosa canina *dog roses, yellow raspberries, currant bushes, and an arched bower of honeysuckle, the sloped path leads down toward a recessed shaded area. Ringed with a thick hedge of masterwort,* Astrantia, *the pale rosy-white flowers enclose a sundial, a recurring element in Finlay's work.*

In the Pompeiian Garden, one of the first areas to be treated by Finlay, lies a small, hidden water feature blanketed with duckweed, Lemna. *Granite blocks ring the well-like fountain, which is planted with* Geranium macrorrhizum, *Siberian iris, and ferns.*

Opposite: A stone path with one of the artist's concrete poems crosses the Middle Pool. By rerouting a hillside spring and the construction of embankments and dams, Finlay created a series of large water features interconnected by streams which enliven the garden. One body of water, The Temple Pool, is adjacent to the artist's house and framed by the Garden Temple. Dedicated to Apollo with the inscription His Music: His Missiles: His Muses, *the former stone outbuilding overlooks the pond. Planted along the water's edge are willows, rowans, irises, and other foliage spilling over in abundance while white-flowering water lilies break the surface and add to the serene atmosphere.*

Pages 110–11: Crossing a bridge carved with Clavdis, *in reference to the pastoral painter Claude Lorrain, the garden opens up to the lake, or Lochan Eck as Finlay has named it. Placed around the large body of water are allusions to the traditions of the landscape garden, with features such as the Ionic capital, sunk in a bed of yellow-flag iris, water buttercups, and forget-me-nots, or the distant column commemorating Finlay's modern-day hero, the French revolutionary Saint-Just. The backdrop of barren moors planted with broom and heather contrasts with the artist's garden and heightens the sensation of paradise contained from within.*

Pages 112–13: Among the tall grasses and dappled shadows, a miniature island in the Upper Pool is planted with alders, encircling a white marble piece titled Silver Cloud. *The secret half-hidden composition, as is true throughout the garden, skillfully uses a few elements to suggest a wealth of imagery. Humility and the sublime are dominant in this magical, peerless landscape.*

JOHN HUBBARD

CHILCOMBE
DORSET / ENGLAND
1965

Opposite: The ancient pair of Irish yews, ringed at the bases with hardy ivy, are on axis with the front door of the manorhouse and provide a dramatic entrance to the series of garden rooms beyond. The lofty yews were one of the few original plantings John Hubbard and his wife found at Chilcombe when they moved to the hillside site.

Tall erect spires of pale mullein, Verbascum, *tower over masses of feverfew,* Chrysanthemum parterium, *and Cape daisies. Each compartamentalized room at Chilcombe has a particular mood conveyed by the choices of plantings and compositions of color. Changing from year to year and at times from the beginning of a season to the next, the bed layouts are constantly modified and altered in the endless quest for yet-untried plant combinations.*

From a simple grid pattern of crisscrossed divisions contained within centuries-old walled enclosures, the American-born painter John Hubbard and his wife, Caryl, have created a series of garden rooms rich in plant diversity, color combinations, and textural composition. Chilcombe, their seventeenth-century Dorset farmhouse complex, sits on the south-facing slope of the Bride Valley, a few miles inland from the English coast. Stylistically, the garden is closely associated with earlier twentieth-century English examples, most notably Vita Sackville-West's Sissinghurst Castle and Lawrence Johnston's Hidcote Manor, although the Hubbards' serial composition of garden experiences defies similarity by way of a richer, more intensified atmosphere. On a far more modest scale than its two legendary counterparts, Chilcombe still remains a high-maintenance and demanding design, a garden that creeps down the acute slope and at each step is explosive in its visual impact.

Chilcombe is characterized by a succession of geometric-shaped beds that disappear beneath the multitude of flowering shrubs, hardy and tender half-hardy perennials densely planted within the graphic compartmentalized framework. The structural grid or framework consists of ancient stone walls, rusticated trellises, tall espaliered apple and pear trees, and a hedge of clipped hornbeam, holly, and yew. Punctuating the rooms are towering poles of honeysuckle and Scarlet runner beans, arched bowers weighed down with clematis and climbing roses, and spires of dark and mysterious Irish yew pillars. It is a garden of focused visual compositions on an intimate, microcosmic scale. The visitor quickly becomes a part of this closed-in world, engulfed within the bursting vegetation which is cultivated to a point of perfection.

Chilcombe is a major source of inspiration and subject matter in Hubbard's expressionistic canvases. Self-described as acts of capturing "the experience of a place," the painter's canvases are charged with dramatic, provocative strokes. Born in the United States in 1931, Hubbard spent three years in Japan, working for military counterintelligence, where he was exposed to Oriental art and the Chinese school of painting in particular. On returning to New York in 1956 he studied at the Arts Students League with the American Abstract Expressionist Hans Hofmann for two years before embarking for Europe. Settling on the Dorset coast in 1961, the artist, married with two children, has for over twenty years cultivated the Chilcombe garden as a cornerstone for this work.

Central to Hubbard's work is the duality of inner and outer, the emergence of space opening outward or narrowing inward. He describes two types of landscape as existing in his paintings and drawings: the interior and the exterior, the closed-in and the opened-up. The Chilcombe garden directly demonstrates the painter's concentration on spirituality. The overabundant, exuberant plantings are prescribed within their small-scaled garden rooms, allowing the eye to closely focus in and observe their particular characteristics and subtle compositional qualities singularly or in relation to other groupings. Colors are organized in tonal gamuts which strengthens their concentrated intensity. Set against the diffused coastal light, colors are even more intense, such as Hubbard's painting of flame-colored crocosmia underplanted with scarlet nasturtiums. Chilcombe is not, however, a garden of violent clashes of contrasting color combinations nor broad sweeps of single plant varieties; rather it is composed of subtle and diversified tones and plantings. It remains a visually arresting and stimulating garden powerful in its ardent array of color and plant variety. Chilcombe's Englishness lies in its richness of plants employed, refined combinations, and spatial divisions, yet John Hubbard moves it beyond this designation or definition with a powerful force and individual eye to create a garden modern in its method set within a familiar context.

The strong bones or geometric framework of Chilcombe can be clearly read from the top-floor windows of the house which overlooks the sloped site. Old stone walls, espaliered apple trees, and a thick, double tapestry hedge composed of holly, copper beech, and hornbeam all define the structural layout of this garden. Vertical punctuations of Irish yew, Taxus baccata *'Stricta Fastigiata', acacias, and poplars provide height and dramatically enliven the small enclosures, as do rusticated archways, wooden tripods, or iron supports, which are overplanted with intertwining roses, clematis, and honeysuckle.*

*A pair of spiral-like Irish yews lend architectural defini-
tion to the entrance of an enclosed space, which is
planted in varying shades of blues, pinks, and purples
and animated with strong dashes of white. The infusion
of color contrasts with the pastoral views of the distant
rolling countryside and sea beyond.*

Characteristic of the densely rich plantings of the exterior rooms at Chilcombe, the painter John Hubbard and his wife have created an abundant casualness which results from the wide juxtaposition of color and texture, such as the red nasturtiums and crocosmia purple toad flax Linaria purpurea.

Overleaf: A corner of the cobbled garden, named for the cobbled stone path that bisects the enclosure. The cottage-style massings of hollyhocks, white lilies, assorted poppies, penstemon, purple sage, and lamb's ears in the foreground are characteristic of the painter's garden style. The heady combinations of hardy and tender plants tightly set within the frame of espaliered apple trees, cloaked in purple clematis, reflect the artist's love for a superabundance of color.

BETTY DI ROBILANT

PORTO ERCOLE
TUSCANY / ITALY
1965

Opposite: Di Robilant transformed the former paddock area between her house and painting studio into an enclosed garden filled with color. Over the years she has radically changed the layout from an informal jun-glelike setting with a winding X-shaped path to its cur-rent design of four symmetrically aligned squares. Large potted lemon trees and a variety of herbs, such as rosemary, thyme, lavender, and mint, are set within each of the raised beds. Like miniature outposts of for-mality, small clipped boxwood are lined along the beds, interspersed with potted deep purple fuchsias and zonal pelargoniums in brilliant red.

Betty di Robilant employs evergreen laurel clipped into a variety of forms, including the arched portal marking the entryway to the artist's house.

In this Italian garden, just outside the Tuscan seaside village of Porto Ercole, a directness of spirit and uncluttered simplicity exist. Employing such architectural vocabulary as solid hedges, stone terraces, and crisp lines, Betty di Robilant's garden is anything but stiff or formal; rather it is a place of easy intimacy. Working with the ancient garden lexicon of cypress trees, olive groves, fragrant myrtle, boxwood, rosemary bushes, and lemon trees, di Robilant has created a series of serene encounters, visually and spiritually. Although di Robilant claims continual indecision or doubt concerning a certain plant or new layout, her artistically acute vision has charted a course that she has continuously followed over the years and that has resulted in pure and straightforward evolving design. The artist's strong leanings toward classicism is translated into contemporary terms by the creation of her very modern compositions.

When di Robilant first came across the property in 1965, the sloped site protected from the icy northern winds suited her primary demands for full southern sun. Light is vitally important for the painter and reveals itself in both her garden and artistic work. Gathering various elements from her garden such as datura, iris, or lily, the artist draws a preliminary portrait of her individual object and then abstracts the essence of her initial rendering. Her large-scale watercolors are filled with a luminosity and generosity that are equaled in her verdant outdoor compositions. In her garden, one moves with heightened feeling from bright sun to dappled shade to darkened shadow to light again. As if to emphasize further this radiance, di Robilant has created a number of features that capture the sensations of light. Overhead canopies of wisteria pergolas filter the bright Italian sunshine, creating speckled patterns while dark laurel hedges absorb the forceful rays. Cast against the cool, inviting velvet lawns are the shimmery reflections of di Robilant's sixteen-tree olive grove. This succession of optical experiences blends into the next and subtly transforms the contemplative all-green garden.

Working with a difficult climate—bitter winters paired against hot, dry summers—the artist has referred to native plant varieties and simplified combinations with great success. An old barn, and now the painter's studio, was annexed to the house by means of a walled patio. After unsuccessful attempts to create a balmy microclimate for growing scented jasmines, gardenias, and mandevillas, the enclosed garden is now planted with hardier varieties. Four raised beds are centrally marked with large lemon trees grown in Tuscan terra-cotta pots, which are moved for protection in winter. Engulfing the quadrant layout is a swirling tide of summer annuals, such as cosmos, nicotiana, zinnias, and blue salvias. Trained up posts and interwoven with grapevines are the bluish-white star-shaped flowers of the potato vine, *Solanum jasminoides,* mixed with creamy white blossoms of *Clematis* 'Henryi' and *C. jackmanii* 'Alba'. Along the warmer south-facing walls are Cooper's Burmese rose, *Rosa cooperi,* with its milky blossoms, which fade to a white with spotted pink. Other roses include the single pure white flowers of the evergreen *Rosa bracteata,* which is intertwined with the white blossoming Bengal clockvine *Thunbergia grandiflora.*

Classical poetry, ancient Greek and Roman authors, and her own fellow gardeners are di Robilant's primary sphere of stimulation in the formation of her garden. Descriptions of Pliny's fields of mauve violets or Charles de Noaille's humble dissertations on compositional sensations are two of the many inspirational catalysts behind the artist's creative process. As a gardener learns from examination, experience, and labor, di Robilant scrutinizes her own gardens as well as ceaselessly investigating those of others. New ideas can arise, which often result in the moving of plants the way someone else might move furniture, injecting into the garden a sense of continuous change and vitality. This garden, which so expressively evokes the character of its guardian, is a serene place where glimpses of a classical world and the energy and spirit of a new one coexist.

Many of the plant varieties used by the American-born artist once composed ancient Greek and Roman gardens, such as cypress, olive, boxwood, and lemon trees. This classical vocabulary has been reinterpreted by di Robilant. Here, above the pale pink drifts of sour cherry blossoms, the clipped hedge of sweet bay, Laurus nobilis, *forms a strong graphic approach to the artist's property.*

Overleaf: Like all devoted gardeners, di Robilant is constantly devising new concepts to be included in the garden, even though some of these ideas remain dreams, to be endlessly reviewed and perfected. One such unrealized idea was her topiary tennis court. In its place where the grass court, laurel umpire chairs, and bleacher stands were to be, the artist has composed a study of clipped geometric shapes. Cubes, rectangles, parallelograms, and cushioned domes are rendered from sweet bay and set within a parterre of crushed stone. Her great fondness for juxtaposing ordered greenery against Arcadian backdrops produced this composition on the southeastern point of her property, overlooking the idyllic valley landscape that rolls down toward the sea.

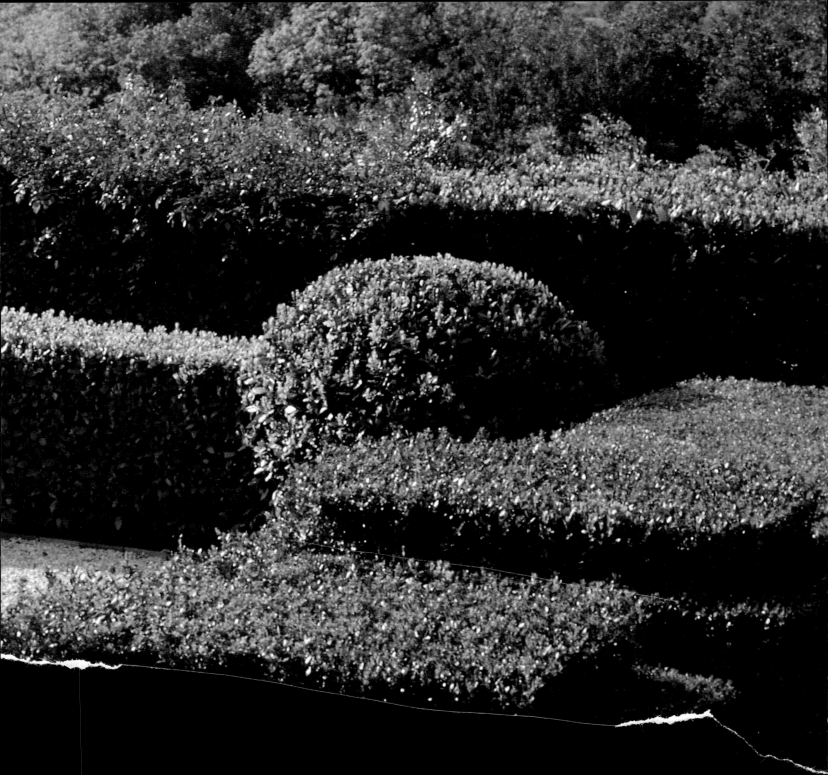

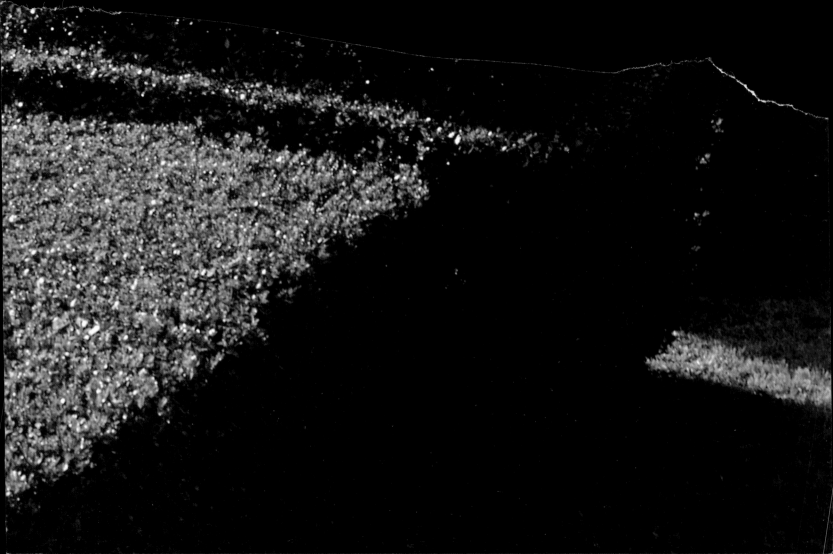

ROBERT DASH

MADOO
SAGAPONACK / LONG ISLAND / NEW YORK
1965

Opposite: Seen from above, the masses of windblown flowers and foliage form waves of changing color that typifies Robert Dash's garden. Vibrant swirls of purple flowering Salvia *enliven this border composed of a wide variety of bulbs and perennials, including peonies, ornamental onions, tall grasses, acanthus, valerian, iris, and buttercups. The clipped waist-high yew hedge screens distant beds and borders.*

Color is employed throughout the garden at Madoo in a variety of ways, including the painted architectural elements such as this door on axis with the bricked path. Repainted at times seasonally, the yellow feature draws the eye across the burgeoning growth that nearly obscures the path, and lures the visitor through the space. The buttercups pick up the yellow of the door and the Johnson's blue geranium provides accent color.

adoo, the American painter Robert Dash's garden, is a paragon of garden design, existing in a league of its own. Although a garden in the truest sense of the word, it challenges any genre classification or definition and forms an altogether original and insurgent model. Madoo has few contemporary equivalents and rivals in spirit the small handful of earlier twentieth-century examples that continue to wield a considerable stronghold on garden criterion today. For over twenty-five years, Robert Dash has created a gardenscape rich and diverse in executed theories and concepts that have progressed beyond its predecessors. A garden of incredible beauty, Madoo has and will continue to exert a significant and profound influence on the approach to future garden design.

Madoo is certainly an interesting place, for it is so abundantly forceful and overpowering in its diversity of impressions. Dash has worked into this heady garden world a strong sense of subtlety and intricacy that counteracts and balances the whole. A garden on a seemingly never-ending quest, it remains neither staid nor contrived, nor even restrained, but rather one concerned with constant change. The overall visual impact is countered at close inspection by concealed touches of intimate delicacy and optical delight. The atmosphere in the painter's garden seems diffused with an eternal lyrical quality that resonates throughout the nearly two-acre site and echoes Dash's dedication to his garden, overshadowed only by his love of painting. The multitude of sensations mirrors the artist's genuine appreciation of the arts; painting, music, literature, poetry, and the classics all contribute to the garden's distinct and original composition.

Dash is a garden's gardener, one who endlessly labors and learns from his land and admittedly so understands more from the dismal failure or unexpected blunder than from an effortlessly successful gesture. In 1965 the artist first took deed to a one-acre windblown farmstead on the rural far-eastern reaches of Long Island in New York State. The flat stretch, wedged between cultivated corn and potato fields, was mainly composed of a grassy, tumbling meadow with a double barn constructed of shipwrecked timber dating to 1740, and two dilapidated shacks. The ceaseless pounding of the Atlantic surf carried throughout the property with occasional glimpses of the ocean. It was a challenging and tempestuous site for a garden and to a degree remains so, where only the hardiest of plant varieties are allowed into the garden schemes.

As a painter, Robert Dash first began as an Abstract Expressionist only to renounce the style later for a more pragmatic, representational approach. He distinguished himself as an American Realist, with the surrounding landscapes as his subject matter. Perhaps reflecting his early attempts to subjugate the boisterous site, Dash painted the ever-changing light and atmosphere of open fields and vegetation. For the past ten years now, the artist has returned to his original style and has produced abstract works that reach deeper into the soul. In later pieces, such as the Darkness series, a multitude of layering, of discernible yet muddy imagery expounds a no-holds-barred, gutsy quality. That very same quality can be said of his garden.

In his early attempts to cultivate the wind-torn site, the painter enclosed the pair of shacks with an L-shaped hall, providing him with a protected inner court. By the second year, the small enclosure had become a verdant jungle with a pond and colorful combinations of snapdragons and cosmos, green zinnias, purple and white petunias, and numerous varieties of daylilies. By the fifth year Dash was hooked and ready to venture out. Detaching the smaller of the two barns, he maneuvered it across the property to the farthest side. A pair of living and work quarters were set up in each, one studio for the winter months and the other for the summer. Tall, closely planted thick hedges of privet, Russian olive, and black pine went in to screen out the Atlantic gales and over the years, many have been limbed up, exposing their twisted dark trunks.

Like any truly interesting garden experience, Dash's garden complex is in a constant state of flux. The artist's bold use of color, as seen here with the purple bench in a surround of evergreen foliage, magnolias, and Baptisia australis, *and his imaginative, frequently modified planting combinations, attest to his ability to transpose the garden vernacular into a contemporary art form. Over the years, Madoo has become a paramount garden to visit, and one that has altered our perceptions of what a garden is and can be. Madoo will be preserved for the future under the auspices of the Garden Conservancy, a group dedicated to the preservation of unique American gardens.*

Madoo is about the mystery of discovery, an adventurous labyrinth for the visitor, as experienced upon arrival, when even the car park offers little in the way of introducing one to the garden. Numerous possibilities become apparent as pathways and garden gates come into focus and one feels like a child again as the adventure begins. The vivid garden posts and garden benches are brightly painted chrome yellow or lime or purple, announcing the colors of a truly individual garden ideal. Madoo is a madcap place where large, river-washed white stones crunch underfoot and tall outcroppings of pink cleomes shoot up from the gravel below. Dash has made a garden that initially appears comprehensible and seemingly simple, yet with each step the possibilities of direction and combinations of plants, of form and color open on to more variation. At every step there are alternate routes to take, and some which require doubling back. The seeming casualness of the garden belies juxtapositions of striking or subtle associations, such as the snow white *Clematis* 'Duchess of Edinburgh' interlaced among the frail pearly petals of a massive *Rosa* 'Double de Corbert'.

Color from nature's palette or the artist's are routinely mixed together as all the wooden garden features are painted in different hues throughout the seasons. A fenced vegetable patch with diagonal bands for beds and brick paths is reinforced with delphiniums and roses popping up among the cardoons, chives, and purple basil. An open grassy meadow, thick with goldenrod left uncut and tall in late summer, is planted intermittently with peonies, broom, and daylilies with scatterings of thistle and rue creating a subtle and rich tapestry effect. A large pond that is rendered nearly invisible through the thickets of iris and bog plants is overshadowed at one end by a viewing pavilion, an ode to the mysteries of the Far East. At another end of the garden an intense violet-painted octagonal gazebo is set near a dreamy grove of stunted ginkgo trees, their lateral branches spreading out from the topped tree crowns. A vast bed of Rugosa roses and ornamental grasses, kept in perpetual motion from the light-filled sea breezes, sways against the dramatic skyscape beyond. Leading out to the property's far reaches is an impressive perspective of a 120-foot arched allée of metal hoops, which march on in axial lineation from the winter house and are overplanted with a Dash favorite, the Dortmund climbing rose. Madoo is a garden where plants as diverse as berrybushes, clematis, or coral bells, once proved sturdy and strong enough for the rough-and-tumble climate, are employed as screens or hedges, accents to evergreens, or edging along a stony path. Likewise, herbs such as basil or strawberries are given equal consideration to Dash's favorites "Nepalese columbines" and *Lamium* × *maculatum* 'White Nancy'.

In a world where conformity equals acceptance, Madoo cries out. It has an individualism that is so very important and of such an alluring brilliance that one can only stand in awe.

Opposite: From a swampy site, Dash has created an Oriental-inspired scene, with the use of such trees as blue cedar and magnolias. Masses of plants, such as Lythrum *purple strife, wisteria, daylilies, and iris, are used to surround the edge of the pond.*

The artist's summerhouse is visible behind the meadow. Nearly engulfed in vegetation, the former barn is cloaked in climbing roses and clematis which seem to anchor the structure to the site, while columnar red cedars, Juniperus virginiana, *Scotch broom, wild phlox, peonies, and spirea add color and form to the tall grass meadow.*

From the swampy meadow that borders one side of the summerhouse, Dash has carved out a cut grass seating area, protected from ocean breezes. Finely mowed paths meander throughout the artist's property revealing features such as the pond, vegetable garden, rose-covered arbors, or ginkgo tree thickets.

Pages 136–37: The painter uses quick strokes of variegated foliage and splashes of color to enliven areas or underline broad statements. Here the feathery, creamy colored Aruncus dioicus marks the termination point of the long sweep of low yew hedges that flank one entrance to the garden. Edged in variegated Lamium × maculatum 'White Nancy', the wide grass path contrasts with the variety of walkways Dash has mapped out for the visitor to follow.

Pages 138–39: Dash produces bold visual surprises by massing together a few elements or contrasting a variety of shrubs, vines, and perennials. Here, drifts of yellow star-shaped Allium moly and beebalm blend with the erect spikes of purplish-blue flowers of Salvia.

CLAUDE AND FRANÇOIS-XAVIER LALANNE

URY / FRANCE
1967

Opposite: Giant clouds of sea kale, Crambe cordifolia, *animate the large vegetable beds that are interspersed with bright red poppies, blue delphiniums, or leeks.*

Under the shade of the grapevine pergola, the elements of dream and reality coexist. The dreamlike atmosphere is derived from the unchecked growth that the couple encourage in their Île-de-France property. Flowering shrubs are planted along the walled divisions, which include Magnolia grandiflora, *forsythias, philadelphus, and viburnums, along with dogwood and ash trees.*

Appearing as in a child's fairy tale, this garden lies on the outer reaches of a legendary royal hunting forest. It is a place of romantic enchantment where the artists Claude and François-Xavier Lalanne live and work. Protected within the high-walled confines of their nineteenth-century former dairy farm on the outskirts of Fontainebleau, the French couple have united both tangible and fanciful metaphors in order to create their dreamlike domain. Partially a workshop and laboratory and also a place for the numerous organic elements required for their sculptures, the garden is a pivotal point of inspiration for their work. This intimate world is where the amalgamations of animal, vegetable, and mineral are unified to form two totally personal artistic expressions.

Art historians and critics alike often quibble when attempting to categorize the Lalannes. Are they sculptors or decorative artists, garden designers or urbanists, craftsmen, artisans, architects, or simply magicians? In the end, the Lalannes—as they are interchangeably known—are all of these. Their art, they believe, should be lived with, utilized in daily life, have the capacity to touch a humorous chord, and above all, to be enjoyed. They continue on—new ideas inspire new projects, which beget new horizons to be explored. Their close attention to the various technical skills involved in producing their art is serious, and the love of what they do, whatever shape or form it may take, is plainly clear in each individual piece.

Claude Lalanne works primarily in bronze, using a century-old molding process called galvano-plasticism, which allows her to reproduce precise phantasmagorical configurations. Since her first Paris show in 1964, Claude has merged artistic beauty and authority with an imaginative playfulness and humorous wit. For example, a tempting bronze apple bares a pair of smirking lips, or a minute snail creeps along, aided by two human fingertips, or a sinuous love seat composed of cow parsnip stocks is interwoven with a backrest of ribbed hosta leaves. Her work contains an innocence and joyfulness that reveal the often forsaken pleasures that can be experienced when the imagination is allowed to run free.

Like his wife, François-Xavier incorporates the zoological alphabet into his sculptural pieces. Employing a wide variety of materials, including bronze or steel, stone, and wool, his welded pieces and sculpted works project a strong sense of the make-believe and fantastic. Overall, they convey tranquility and inner peace. Many of Lalanne's works, regardless of size or scale, suggest monumentality; their stylized lines and dignity bring to mind the graphic forms of ancient Egyptian art as well as the refined, sublime works of Constantin Brancusi. It is no surprise that both were major influences in François-Xavier's early years: Lalanne lived next door to the great sculptor in Montparnasse and he also worked as a guard in the Louvre's department of antiquities. But the predominant response to Lalanne's work is sheer delight. His imaginative constructions are varied and surprising: a giant fish-tailed feline spreads open to reveal a full-stocked bar; a gorilla is also a fiery potbellied stove; a donkey is a desk; and a grazing flock of sheep doubles as comfortable cushioned stools. For both artists, their labors are destined far from the seriousness of the art-museum pedestal, but rather for a common and useful purpose, however unorthodox.

Claude created the delightful Children's Garden for the City of Paris in 1981 as well as outdoor furniture for the Wallace Foundation in Williamsburg, Virginia. François-Xavier, beginning with his 1973 unrealized Dragon Garden in the Côte d'Azur, was responsible for the fountain and topiaries for the City Hall in Paris and the area around the Les Halles complex. Although the artists work independently, they have occasionally collaborated on some garden commissions. They produced designs for a park in New Orleans, sculptural fountains in Santa Monica, California, and their most ambitious project yet, the gardens for the Center of European Education outside Fontainebleau.

The Lalannes' walled garden complex displays the identity of its owners without hesitation. It is not easily imitated, for so much of its composition relies on the artist's response to changes in nature. The imagery—both natural and applied—fits into a casual layout. Be-

*Inside the towering vine-clad metal garden pavilion a
lacelike tracery effect is silhouetted against the sky. Both
the grapevine tendrils and foliage are other examples of
the vegetation that Claude Lalanne has drawn and used
in her work.*

tween the two artists, the garden supports an astonishing array of animal forms and
vegetables, which they have assimilated into their work over the years. Claude gathers
ginkgo, cabbage, fennel bulbs, and iris leaves from the garden for her artistic meta-
morphoses, in addition to the snails, apples, dragonfly wings, and rabbits she uses. François-
Xavier ventures further afield: his cows, donkeys, carp, ducks, even gorillas, hippos,
ostriches, and sardines come from sources well beyond his immediate surroundings.

In comparison to the harvested wealth of stimulation that is culled by the artists, their
garden is in fact unusually small. The nearly one-acre property lies south of Paris, in the Île-
de-France village of Ury, and is distinguished from the neighboring buildings in summer by
the towering hollyhocks that shoot up along the walls fronting the street. Within, stone
dividers break up the farmstead into three basic enclosures: two courtyard spaces—one for
each of the artists and their respective studios—and a large central garden and greenhouse.

The middle garden, which is flanked for balance on either side by each of the artist's
studios, is equally divided into lawn and cultivated plots. During a given year, François-
Xavier's stone sheep might graze under the apple trees awaiting shipment, or a cluster of
Claude's flag iris-leaf bronze chairs may be interspersed on the occasionally mowed grass. A
lofty metal armature—a simple cube with a pyramidal top—stands in a corner of shrubs and
in the summer is entirely shrouded by hops and grapevine, providing the ideal spot for hot,
lazy afternoons.

Unlike most gardeners, the Lalannes have a great reverence for the surprises that spring up with self-sown plants and weeds. The garden is crowded with an abundance of flowering shrubs, vines, perennials, and biannuals, many of which come back season after season. Adjacent to a vegetable and flower patch is a stretch of grass dotted with apple trees. After the apple blossoms flower in early summer, the trees are completely covered in cascades of climbing roses.

Large beds, with a central walk that tends to become overgrown by midsummer, are filled with rows of vegetables and herbs. Leek and cabbage, fennel, French beans, and strawberries are interspersed with towering spires of blue delphiniums and pale hollyhocks. Bright red poppies sown years ago have invaded the area as have Queen Anne's lace and sweet pea. A new addition by Claude Lalanne is a seating area centered within the vegetable garden and enclosed on two sides with fencelike apple espaliers and morning glories twisting up the trunks. Large, white flowering mock orange and viburnums form a dense backdrop against the old stone wall and street behind. Grapevines are permitted to grow the way they naturally tend—which is every which way and every direction. When weeds appear in the rows of flowers and vegetables, or invade a stone foundation or shrubbery border, they are noticed more often than not for their beauty than for their disgrace. While the effect of all this growth can be overwhelming at times, particular flowers or herbs and vegetables can be plucked for consumption or artistic use without the slightest disturbance to the whole composition. Tiny strawberries and nasturtium mounds thrive at the bases of hollyhocks and iris. A great number of the plants are permitted to carry out their full cycle from flower to seed to regeneration. Chives, leeks, and cabbages transform themselves into rarely seen tall stalks of gigantic proportions.

A child's paradise, this compound of old stone walls, abundant garden yards, and leafy tunneled passageways and portals is imbued with an air of romantic abandonment and nonchalance. For the visitor, the Lalannes' garden represents complete enchantment. For the artists, the importance of their garden is paramount, the visual link between reality and dream. One awaits with great interest to witness the next inspired transformation in this most beautiful paradise.

A view from the central garden into Claude Lalanne's studio courtyard. The bronze gate was cast from twigs found on the property. The stone wall, covered in hop vines and giant cow parsnip, Heracleum laciniatum, *is hidden beneath the tumbling growth.*

Overleaf: The abundant growth covering this pergola is carefully pruned grapevine, which achieves a tentlike effect for this outdoor seating area.

JOAN MITCHELL

VÉTHEUIL / FRANCE
1968

*Opposite: Behind Joan Mitchell's house and just off the
kitchen was the painter's private garden, which only she
tended. Gardening was peaceful recreation for Mitchell;
at times she would even weed late at night, aided by
outdoor lights. Here, the steep staggered terraced plots
are filled with wallflowers along with her other favorites, African marigolds, yellow coreopsis, and orange
zinnias. As a gardener, she was excited by bold, gutsy
associations of color, form, and texture derived from
commonly available plant varieties.*

*The distant bell tower of the twelfth-century Gothic
church of Vétheuil was often painted by Claude Monet
when he briefly lived in the gardener's cottage on what is
now Joan Mitchell's property. The almost one-acre
walled vegetable garden layout existed in its present
form when the artist purchased the estate in 1968.
Flowering lavender bushes are intermixed with rows of
vegetables and cut flowers.*

Until her sudden death in the autumn of 1992, the American painter Joan Mitchell made her home in the village of Vétheuil, less than an hour's drive from Paris, in the Île-de-France region. The small community built around an imposing Gothic church hugs the bank of the river Seine, a scene relatively unchanged over the past one hundred years. In looking at the view from her house, the artist would refer to the panorama across the river and poplar trees as her own personal "view of Delft." The analogy with Vermeer's only known landscape painting had particular meaning for Mitchell, as both sites were honored with a mystical quality of light. Mitchell's property, perched high atop the village and river, was where the artist lived with her dogs and painted for nearly twenty-four years within her two-acre garden compound. Although she often claimed to be an outsider and to feel at home nowhere—a sentiment commonly shared by expatriates—the Chicago-born painter cherished her garden setting that seemed so perfectly in accordance with the way she lived and worked.

The hillside property was shaped and tended to with many of the same characteristics that come to mind when describing Mitchell's Abstract Expressionist work. In both, the grand flourishes and passions are subject to the sense of discipline and authority that prevails. Mitchell spoke of herself as a controlled artist, one who felt creative freedom through reflection and hard work. Her garden speaks of the same rigor and vitality. In this large expanse, great variations are encountered, just as they are in Mitchell's canvases and pastels. Perhaps the most striking attribute seen in both the artist's work and her garden is a submission to order and stability. This kind of rigor in the garden is not expressed by perfect symmetry nor by a balance conventionally associated with French classical landscapes, but rather by the kind of attention usually reserved for much smaller garden plots. Whether typified by the shaded, steep gravel walk that leads from street to house or the apple orchard terrace, the casual atmosphere of the place comes from Mitchell's respect for nature and the land.

The garden in Vétheuil was a great source of inspiration in Joan Mitchell's work. Although she did not paint the orderly vegetable rows, the leafy shadows from the great linden that shaded her house, or the small fenced garden she herself tended, the painter strove to recall the visual memories of such experiences as well as her memories of the water and the landscapes of her childhood and early adult days on the East Coast. Her thickly painted canvases and textural pastels evoke the color and light in her garden.

Possibly the most fascinating area of Mitchell's property is the vegetable garden with its narrow, geometric-shaped plots tended to by her gardener, the octogenarian Monsieur Jean. Surrounded by high masonry walls and enclosed within by low espaliered fences of apple and pear and thick hedges of red currant and raspberries, the meticulous and painstakingly cultivated rows upon rows of vegetables are interplanted with seasonally flowering perennials and annuals. American corn, potatoes, strawberries, fennel, parsley, and carrots are interspersed with dahlias, roses, sunflowers, and iris, an example of the French tradition of cultivating for both purpose and pleasure. This symphony of color, texture, and varying shapes and forms is certainly joyous, but it also shows a kind of repetitive devotion, bordering on folly. Like vivid ribbons or blocks of pure color, the vegetable garden was the artist's great pleasure and a place where she would come and sit to reflect on her work. Joan Mitchell's attachment to the centuries-old French gardening tradition and everything it represents is part of the sublime seduction of this garden. One can only hope this spectacular place continues to exert its specialness for many years to come.

A ribbonlike row of iris edges one side of the vegetable plot, backed by small fruit trees and towering lindens. Much of the two-acre property was divided into special areas: the vegetable garden; the apple orchard with roses trained up the trunks; the shady house terrace; and her painting studio enclosure, which was planted with great clumps of peonies and iris amid large drifts of evergreen junipers and yuccas.

A view of the terrace planted with fruit trees, overlooking the river Seine below. Mitchell had trained climbing roses to grow up the trunks of the fruit trees.

Opposite: Under the shadow of towering horse chestnut trees, a boxwood-lined hedge defines the gravel path, which leads from the artists's house to the large vegetable garden beyond.

Pages 154–55: Joan Mitchell often referred to the "color feeling" of her garden and the surrounding fields that inspired many of her works. Rather than paint a specific image observed in the landscape, the artist strove to repeat the feeling or sensation of her land. Against a tall hedgelike row of American corn, the vivid feathery shoots of asparagus are enlivened with red currant bushes.

HIROSHI TESHIGAHARA

KYOTO AND TOKYO / JAPAN
1980S

AND

CHAUMONT / FRANCE
1992

Opposite: The artist often works with bamboo in creating installation pieces. For the Fall 1992 garden exposition held at Chaumont in the Loire Valley, Hiroshi Teshigahara created an extraordinary tunnel of split and sanded bamboo canes that curved within a small confined space. The flooring is carpeted with pine needles.

A side view of the tsuboniwa *garden designed by Teshigahara in Kyoto. The tied rock symbolizes no entry and signals the visitor not to proceed any farther.*

The diverse artistic achievements of Hiroshi Teshigahara reflect the wide variety of contemporary expressions that have developed during the course of art in the twentieth century. Within the expanded definitions that categorize an artistic creation, such manifestations as film, temporary installations, or performance pieces have become accepted alternatives to the traditional mediums of painting and sculpture. Artists mirror their surrounding environment, and certain contemporary compositions have come to reflect the changes and complexities of the current world.

Born in 1927, Hiroshi Teshigahara is one of Japan's foremost artists who bridges the traditions of his country's rich cultural heritage with contemporary concerns; the result produces modern expressions depicting man's intervention and transfiguration of nature. Teshigahara first worked as a painter before turning to filmmaking in the early sixties.

Perhaps best known for the award-winning *The Women in the Dunes*, he has also directed both opera and theater productions. Inspired by ceramics in the early seventies, Teshigahara founded the Sogestu Tobo Kiln in 1973, where he devoted himself to producing pottery objects unencumbered by traditional forms. More significantly, Hiroshi Teshigahara is the son of Sofu Teshigahara, who founded the influential Sogestu School which teaches Japanese garden design and most notably ikebana, the art of flower arranging with respect to form, balance, and harmony. Since 1980, Teshigahara has succeeded his father in the position of headmaster, or *iemoto*.

Working with the principles of ikebana, Teshigahara has applied his own ideas about artistic expression, resulting in the creation of numerous temporary installations. Frequently composed of bamboo, these works are shown both in art galleries and museums, such as the Centre Pompidou in Paris. For the artist, the transformation of plants gathered from nature represents man's intention to control and form the natural world. In each of Teshigahara's three-dimensional compositions—from the large-scale works to the temporary or miniature-scale renditions—the concept of nature confronted and transformed is realized. By taking a pure plant material, such as bamboo for instance, and manipulating it somehow—by bending, carving, molding, or splitting it—the artist takes it to its most extreme point, one of virtual abstraction.

In Teshigahara's work there exists a dynamic tension and spirited energy in his various garden compositions, which powerfully shape a visitor's sense of space. As our own world grows smaller or more accessible, and the natural environment becomes increasingly fragile, Teshigahara's garden works project the importance of safeguarding the powerful sensations that a given landscape can evoke.

For this commercial site in downtown Tokyo, Teshigahara sculpted the massive stone form and planted dwarf variegated bamboo. Set within a wide gravel bed that represents peaceful waters, the artist incorporates his concept of two opposing elements of nature, in this case stone and dwarf bamboo, to create a harmonious atmosphere.

Overleaf: Teshigahara transformed this narrow Kyoto courtyard into a miniature tsuboniwa, or pocket garden, which he intended to be viewed from inside a building. A green moss "river" seems to flow through the granite paved space and changes according to the seasons, from a vivid green in spring to a rusty brown in winter. The miniature ikebana landscape is changed periodically, with cut branches of peach or Cornus mas branches, as seen here, in spring to tall grasses or bamboo stalks in winter.

NIKI DE SAINT-PHALLE

GIARDINI DEI TAROCCHI
CAPALBIO / ITALY
1980

Opposite: A twisting fountain jet by Jean Tinguely animates the water basin at the base of the cascade that washes down from the High Priestess and Magician, two of the twenty-two Major Arcana attributes of the Tarot that Niki de Saint-Phalle incorporated into her garden.

The Giardini dei Tarocchi is rare among contemporary landscapes and rivals such extraordinary places as Villa Orsini at Bomarzo or the Désert de Retz, with their stone monsters and follies.

Along the coastal road that heads north linking Rome with the town of Grosseto, one suddenly notices the blinding reflections from an undulating silvery-gray olive grove. Glittering in the sun like a thousand beacons of light is Niki de Saint-Phalle's Tarot Garden. The French-born artist has created an amazing visionary landscape carved out of the cultivated Tuscan landscape,.

One of the lessons learned from developments in art, and most notably through the works of the Surrealists, is the powerful force of the unconscious. This realm of the subliminal has been explored by more than a handful of daring artists. Among them is Niki de Saint-Phalle, whose brand of perception consists of looking at the hidden world of dreams. Her continued investigation of this fantasy world produces works of art that seem universal; the whimsical gaiety and childlike innocence of her sculptural figures rendered in contemporary mediums are creations that remain familiar and pure.

The Giardini dei Tarocchi, conceived and labored on continuously since 1980, is the culmination of the artist's lifelong desires. Having wished for years to construct a garden close to the sea in Tuscany, Niki de Saint-Phalle found this hillside situated on a private estate owned by friends. Within its protected confines de Saint-Phalle was allowed total freedom to create, literally, the landscape of her dreams. The secluded former quarry site yielded sweeping views across the grassy fields to the shimmering Mediterranean coastline. Financed entirely by the artist herself, the garden has taken form over the past thirteen years with the continued addition of her architectonic sculptures based on the ancient Tarot, and the twenty-two essential archetypal images of the Major Arcana.

Although this is not a garden in any conventional sense, there is something strangely familiar in its evocations of the dream world. The artist's nonacademic training has enriched this place with a sense of freedom and flexibility. This timeless world includes grotesque, terrifying follies, such as the early fifteenth-century Bosco di Bomarzo, the layered imagery of Mayan and Hindu temples, and monumental Egyptian edifices. Another influence on de Saint-Phalle was Park Güell, in Barcelona, designed by the Spanish architect Antonio Gaudí. Employing for the first time in her work the Gaudían vocabulary of brightly colored glazed ceramics, de Saint-Phalle has taken the context further to include reflective mirror fragments and a vast array of rainbow-hued hand-blown glass for the surface treatments.

As if forced to follow a predestined route, the artist created a complex system of pathways that link the various half-hidden follies. Approaching the garden from above, the land slopes down and underneath the dappled shade canopies of olive and live oak trees. The underbrush becomes quite sparse and one has the impression of walking in a totally foreign land as de Saint-Phalle's manufactured hallucinations slowly begin appearing. The first response, one of trepidation as one meekly confronts the mystical, over-scaled configurations, quickly transpires to a feeling of discovery and ceaseless curiosity which drives one on. Birds and snakes, humans, animals, and free-form shapes transpose themselves into The Empress, The Tower, or the personification of Justice, representatives of the Major Arcana. Like a child set free to run, one darts in and out, up and down amid the secret labyrinth of staircases, passageways, viewing terraces, and hidden chambers. The organic curved surfaces become mirrors of the light and shadow of the surrounding natural world as well as of visitors passing by. This sense of perpetual motion and constant animation created by the wind, sunlight, cascading water, and sculptures creates a greatly seductive atmosphere. This garden transports the visitor far beyond a real world to a place where individual experience and memory condition each step. Joie de vivre carries from one artistic interpretation of the Major Arcana to the next. These garden follies take us back in subconscious time and, like Alice wandering in Wonderland, we rediscover those forgotten pleasures of life.

To inhabit one's dreams is the extraordinary ability to begin the process of uncovering the mazelike secrets of the soul. Composed of a multitude of personal visions and symbolic metaphors, Niki de Saint-Phalle's garden emerges as a second, if not a first, "true" reality.

As one drives along the coastal road linking Rome with Grosseto, a glittering apparition makes its presence known. This is Niki de Saint-Phalle's Tower, situated in the Tarot Garden. The Tower, which represents loss and calamity, is entirely sheathed in cut mirror and rises from the olive grove.

Overleaf: An interlocking system of pathways connects each of the architectonic sculptures, passing through areas of open sky and deep shadow.

SANDRO CHIA

CASTELLO ROMITORIO
MONTALCINO / ITALY
1986

Opposite: A majestic ivy-clad oak towers above one of the steep stone embankments Sandro Chia created while terracing the hillside for his vineyards. The ancient tree, like a number of other landscape features, stands alone as if to defy the rigors of the mountaintop terrain.

Behind the cube-shaped castle a stable courtyard was annexed in the seventeenth century. Protected from the prevailing strong winds, the enclosed courtyard is poetically transformed with the sonorous effects of dripping water from the fountain trough, set against the harsh stone facade.

This austere and formidable landscape best illustrates the fundamental concept of what makes a garden. Here, in the rolling wooded hillsides and vineyards of Tuscany, the Florentine-born painter Sandro Chia has created a landscape that challenges contemporary classification. In a little over six years, the artist has carved away, replanted, and simplified a terrain that embodies the bare-bones definition of a garden. This plot of land, consisting of cultivated forest groves, fruit tree orchards, grapevines, vegetables, and herbs, compels the visitor to confront the natural world.

For six months of the year Sandro Chia leaves his New York City studio and returns to Castello Romitorio, located outside the town of Montalcino, an hour's drive south of Siena. Translated as "the isolated place," the thirteenth-century fortified castle of Castello Romitorio is perched high atop a windswept site; seen from afar the cube-shaped stone stronghold looks like a child's building block left behind somewhere. After purchasing the abandoned 200-acre property in 1986, the artist restored the interior of the imposing structure and began a program to augment the dramatic severity of the landscape, thus intensifying its inherently Tuscan character. The austere lines of the unadorned exterior facades became more pronounced when Chia removed former traces of flower beds and self-germinated vegetation from around the fortress walls. By seeding a wide lawn of grass, the artist has dislodged the massive edifice farther from the surroundings, distancing the castle from the wilderness backdrop. The leveled green plateau is framed by a dense, low hedge of Portuguese laurel, *Prunus lusitanica,* that runs from a grove of twisted live oak trees, which enshroud the iron entrance gates. Void of any plantings that might soften the junction between cultivated land and the castle, Chia has created various stone terraced seating areas away from any strong winds in order to catch the warm sun.

Because of the precipitous site, a series of terraces were sculpted from the sheer slopes and planted out. Hidden below the evergreen laurel hedge is a plowed sloped field, which can be accessed by a steep path bordered on either side by large rosemary bushes interspersed with tall grasses and blackberry canes. At the base of the ramp on the closest reaches of the tilled earth are rows laid out with onions, leeks, artichokes, and potatoes. Descending below the vegetable patch are diagonal alignments of fruit trees—apple, pear, cherry, and plum—enlivening the space in an orderly manner.

From the high reaches of the castle, views can be seen of distant knolls, which Chia has cleared to create vineyards. Ten acres spread out across the rolling folds where strings of wooden vertical support posts and gigantic watering hydraulics overshadow the newly trained grapevines. This intentional desire to strip the land of any contemporary notion of garden features has not, however, left the land barren of experiences. A tall chain-link fence surrounding the circumference of the castle has been overplanted with deep green ivies, creating ribbonlike crenelated walls. A sense of the rugged landscape pervades Chia's property, where wide, expressive tilled tracts and vineyards open up or rocky walkways twist and turn along the Tuscan terrain. The simplicity of the artist's landscape and its directness and clarity of spirit recall monastery compounds of the Middle Ages.

Immediately upon arrival at Castello Romitorio one experiences the various forces of nature. In unprotected spots, the sun beats down, or the wind blows almost continuously, requiring Chia to choose plants for their hardiness and rigor. A garden by definition and even more importantly a garden by decision, Sandro Chia's property deliberately acknowledges the powerful will of nature.

From the wooded slopes surrounding his Tuscan castle, Sandro Chia reclaimed nearly 10 acres for the cultivation of Brunello wine grapes. In spring, yellow-flowering wild mustard grows between rows of grapevine supports.

Overleaf: Viewed from the top reaches of Castello Romitorio, the Tuscan valley opens up well beyond the wooded forest. The imposing thirteenth-century fortified castle casts a dark shadow over the fruit tree orchard and olive grove, both planted by the artist. The tilled earth and simple alignments characterize many of the soft-spoken interventions Chia has undertaken, creating the overall stark and contemplative environment.

APRIL GORNIK

SAG HARBOR / LONG ISLAND / NEW YORK
1988

Opposite: Screened from the rest of the garden by a tall privet hedge, a narrow strip of property between the house and the property line has been transformed by Gornik with a bed of perennials. The tapestry effect of roses, daylilies, Ajuga reptans 'Burgundy Glow' and coral bells, is interspersed with towering allium and iris.

Trained against the artist's painting studio, the climbing rose 'Buff Beauty' naturally arches under the heavy weight of its creamy blossoms.

This garden draws from the English landscape vocabulary of striking foliage combinations and muted color associations, and more specifically from the garden principles of Gertrude Jekyll, who employed a wide range of intermixed perennials, flowering vines, and woody shrubs. April Gornik has made selective use of this garden tradition to offer a thoroughly contemporary counterpart, in this case on the far eastern shores of Long Island. Gornik, who purchased this nineteenth-century village house with the painter Eric Fischl, has ventured further into her newly discovered pastime with an increased assurance and even greater authority in recent years.

Much like the artist's paintings, the garden projects harmony and peacefulness, sometimes in startling contrast to the surrounding real world. In her large canvases and diffuse charcoal drawings, Gornik renders landscapes of still waters and sunsets, of luminous horizons or almost surrealist thin rows of trees which seem momentarily captured in time. In her Long Island garden, the artist has created a landscape that, while neither formally structured or patterned by strict lines or geometric configurations, nor characterized by randomly scattered plantings, draws the visitor onward from one visually stimulating area to the next. An undulating mowed lawn spreads out, wrapping around towering hemlocks or wild privet hedges, engulfing the cream-colored house and weathered shed, delineated by a plain picket fence. Acting as a visual focal point is a stone-and-wood painting studio used by Fischl, partly concealed by the cloudlike forms of a perennial bed. There, thick waves of *Baptisia australis, Alchemilla mollis,* and Siberian iris are interspersed with dashes of pale roses and daylilies. Throughout the garden the color schemes tend to be muted tones of pinks, creams, and blues, enlivened with touches of scarlet reds, deep bronzes, or yellow-tinged foliage. In the studio bed drifts of deep blue flowering *Salvia × superba* are interwoven with low silvery foliage of *Stachys byzantina,* or coral-colored *Heuchera × brizoides.*

In one semishady corner, her original circular bed that had been planted with a large collection of old roses proved less than successful, prompting Gornik to edit the varieties and reduce the shape to a smaller square. Many of the roses, which include such favorites as 'New Dawn', 'Buff Beauty', and 'Angel Face', were moved to sunnier beds and trained against walls of trellises. During her early gardening days, the artist would visit other gardens nearby—most notably Robert Dash's—to find out more about plant hardiness and tolerance in the region. Learning that daylilies thrive in the moist Long Island climate, Gornik has since developed an impressive collection of more than one hundred different varieties and hybrids, scattered everywhere within the flowering borders and beds. The wide color range and blooming periods that run from midsummer until fall are carefree and have become a passion of the artist. April Gornik favors 'Niles Crane', 'Chicago Ruby', and 'Baby Talk', as well as other miniature hybrids cultivated by the breeder Pauline Henry. These are interspersed among the clumps of iris, Scotch broom, or shrub roses.

Even more than devotion and vigilance, April Gornik's garden displays what makes any garden good—experimentation and experience.

Scads of daylilies and drifts of Scotch broom grow in one of the colorful beds at the back of April Gornik's property. The range of pink and creamy hemerocallis is enlivened with a strong red variety and the blue-violet balloon flower, Platycodon grandiflorus.

Overleaf: This small herb garden, situated between Eric Fischl's painting studio and the garden shed, is the only concession April Gornik makes to a formal geometric layout. The three-foot-tall bushy, aromatic bergamot, Monarda didyma *'Violet Queen', forms a low backdrop to the garden, and also softens the weathered fence. Profusely flowering 'New Dawn' cascades from the shed, at left, creating a second hedgelike enclosure for the beds of purple sage, dwarf lavender, and thyme. Two miniature dwarf spruce trees add a note of formal symmetry.*

ANNE AND PATRICK POIRIER

TURIN / ITALY
1989

*Opposite: The green marble column was purposely bro-
ken and is in startling contrast to the severe, clean lines
of the metal pergola frame and the marble paneled
retaining wall, which brings to mind Byzantine construction. Japanese wisteria, trained across the top of
the metal grid, is pruned to create a shade canopy while
the long flowering clusters are allowed to cascade down,
providing the garden with one of the few seasonal
splashes of color.*

*Viewed from the second-story window, the mosaic ter-
race composed of black-and-white marble squares was
relaid a number of times before the Poiriers achieved the
undulating movement that reminded them of ancient
Roman and Byzantine pavements.*

Anne and Patrick Poirier's artistic collaborations contain a timeless quality. Drawing from a vocabulary of the ancient world as a metaphor for memory, or the loss thereof, the French couple create works of art that strike a strong emotional cord in a contemporary context. Their sculptural pieces and large-scale outdoor installations have a haunted, inhabited mood that addresses the forgotten or consigned to oblivion, and mirror the loss of civilization as we know it.

Over the years the Poiriers have sketched, recorded, and catalogued such ancient sites as Aphrodisias and Selinute. Their large maquettes of archaeological digs reflect the couple's impressions of such Roman sites as Ostia Antica or Domus Aurea. Over the past twenty years their work has evolved to the point where they have constructed idealized cities, such as the 1990 *Mnemosyne* piece, a gigantic model city based on their concepts of memory and the formation of the mind. The Poiriers have created numerous site-specific sculptures conceived for garden spaces that interpret their regard for antiquity, including *The Fall of the Giants, Promenade Classique,* and *Oculus Memoriae.* Their large-scale works provide the intellectual jolt for an understanding of the link between man and the surrounding natural world. The artists' repeated interventions with the landscape underline their continued discourse with nature; for them the abandonment of previous civilizations equals the abandonment of our contemporary one.

This sensibility is readily observed in this garden in Turin. In 1989 the Poiriers were commissioned to redesign the private site, less than an acre, which commands a dramatic vista overlooking the northern Italian city. So rarely obtained in contemporary garden design, the artists' scheme produced a landscape of striking simplicity. The sculptural elements set within the site evoke a timeless, ethereal sphere. This spiritual transformation heightens the garden's unique quality and increases the sense of surprise and astonishment one experiences upon entering into it.

The garden consists of a number of common features. The simplified terminology of hedges, trees, rolling lawn, sunny terrace, shady pergola, and reflecting pool are used to form a very contemporary perception of a garden. The bold stroke of the 30-meter-long white marble basin runs parallel to the house and the length of the far property line. The shallow shimmering sheet of water counterbalances the vitalized city below and beyond. For an urban dweller, the requirements of a garden space can be very different from those of a rural inhabitant. The power to screen urban chaos is paramount and a key principle the Poiriers incorporated into their design.

The pared-down simplicity of the hillside garden reveals a calm and composed unit. The passage of time is marked by the changing angle of the sun rather than relying on seasonal flowers and foliage. Most of the plants employed in the scheme have a dual purpose: year-round interest and protective, screening qualities. Hardy and urban tolerant evergreens make up the composition with thick, dense hedges of *Quercus ilex,* glossy-leafed *Magnolia grandiflora,* which when tightly planted shield a neighboring roofline, and creeping ivies to soften the stark contours. The thick, white blocks that make up the shallow water feature were hewn from a single, solid slab of Carrara marble. The monumental effect of the pool is further increased by the elongated marble veins that glisten under the waterline, echoing the presence of the architectural element. The miniature row of broken columns was used to evoke a sense of the past and to add a false perspective, thereby increasing the depth of the narrow garden city. At the entrance to the garden, a marble paved terrace was laid out in a pattern recalling ancient city plans or bird's-eye views of archaeological digs. Set atop the grassy knoll that dominates the garden, a black-painted metal pergola frame is supported at one corner by a dark green marble column. The perfectly proportioned shaft was purposely broken by the Poiriers, and serves as a reminder of the fragility of manmade elements.

This tranquil garden beautifully suggests classical order and harmony. Yet its monumental effects and subtle surprises could only be found in contemporary garden design.

The scaled trunks of the two pine trees and a towering chestnut were the only existing features the Poiriers retained before they redesigned this hillside garden. The marble colonnade "ruin" and fluted column fragment typify the French artists' use of classical elements in their work.

Pages 184–85: Differing leaf forms of ivy are trained up a horse chestnut tree trunk and around the column fragment, thus softening the stark lines and adding an air of romanticism. For this city garden the reliance on evergreen plants was of high importance.

Pages 186–87: The perfectly suited scale of the garden elements is always coupled with a practical rationale. For example, the narrow hillside plot was almost doubled in size with the construction of the Carrara marble water feature, which extends outward from the steep slope and runs parallel to the house facade. The diminutive scale of the colonnade creates a false sense of perspective and increases the perceived depth of the garden when viewed from the house.

JEAN-CHARLES BLAIS

VENCE / FRANCE
1990

Opposite: Seen from a terrace above, the Islamic-inspired garden pavilion and geometric beds are wedged between walls of vegetation. Planted with both gray and green santolina, the folly is enhanced with the star-shaped fountain and jet. Hidden under layers of dirt, the bright ceramic tiles, which bring to mind Moroccan motifs, were restored as were those under the pergola.

Concealed treasures are discovered in this hillside garden such as a grottolike fountain, niched in a stone wall, which appears from behind a spray of palm fronds, or the assortment of painted earthenware jars glimpsed above.

Since graduating from the Ecole des Beaux-Arts in 1979, Jean-Charles Blais has emerged as one of the most important young painters in France. The artist uses the back sides of discarded billboard posters as his canvases, which convey textural richness to his figurative compositions. Often painted fragments of a man, a tree, an animal, or a house, Blais's work directly addresses current issues in art.

Originally built in the 1920s by a Frenchman who had lived many years in North Africa, the Moorish-style villa, located in the higher elevations between Nice and Grasse, was entirely disguised beneath a thick blanket of vegetation. Up until Blais's inspection, the exotic character of the architecture and unchecked growth had intimidated most people. Blais, however, felt otherwise. The phenomenal site impressed him, and in the span of one day he decided to purchase the property.

There is a curious phenomenon that occurs when one is confronted with the responsibility of a garden for the first time. The idea of owning a garden can seem daunting, if not intimidating, when faced with its care. Therein lies the powerful seduction. Like alchemy, what had once seemed a mass of indistinguishable plants slowly began to reveal itself to Blais with bewitching appeal. Over a period of time, Jean-Charles Blais became thoroughly engaged in the process of transforming his Provence hillside terrain.

In 1990, the artist began his excavation of the garden, working at the measured pace of an archaeologist. His lack of experience led to some early misadventures, which caused him to revise certain of his plans. The resulting landscape displays an artistic eloquence and purity, which reflect the painter's thoughtful design process. Behind the whitewashed pavilion-like villa, the steep banks have been partially cleared to reveal the remnants of a former garden feature. Giant palm trees spaced in an ordered sequence and occasional stone borders suggested an abandoned series of climbing trails. Instead of obliterating all references to the former garden, Blais chose to adapt his design around the existing structure. Thus, while neither completely restored nor totally dismantled, the phantom of the former pathway remains, and becomes an entirely "new" garden experience.

From the villa's marble-paved terrace, ribbons of grassy levels recede toward an overgrown field, which is bound at the far end by a protective row of trees and rundown stone house. Farther still, the distant Bay of Cannes is visible from the terraces below. Stone paths and flights of steps in mazelike configurations link the series of terraced spaces. The levels vary one from the other; for instance, one contains a glass greenhouse for potted plants while another is planted with massive acanthus beds or long vegetable rows.

Color has been introduced sparingly to great effect by the artist. A double row of peach trees on one terrace creates a pale rosy hue in spring, or in summer a climbing bougainvillea becomes a hot magenta vapor trained up the side of the whitewashed house facade. Strings of multicolored electric bulbs dangle from an allée of metal hoops and are intertwined with rambling roses, creating a nighttime promenade of perfumed scent and radiant gaiety. The sense of frolic and amusement abounds here and one realizes how key it is. Other terraces are vast linear grass lawns that serve no other purpose than as open spaces for occasional recreation or outdoor painting. Preliminary attention had been given to restoring the architecture of the house, the Moorish follies, various water features, and the painting studio located close by. With the bones of the property well in place, Blais was free to think about the garden. Little by little, plants have been added. Newly completed lavender beds and santolina parterres now thrive while other areas remain as they were when the artist first arrived, for want of a better idea. This slackened pace is relaxing and accommodates the special quality of the landscape. The ability and luxury of time, which is as essential to a good garden as soil, sun, or water, is the artist's enjoyment. Under the shade of ancient gnarled live oaks, a mossy path leads past a stone portal to a walled garden, left to its own undisturbed growth. Here, overblown grasses, wildflowers, and a rectangular reflecting tank create an environment that one hopes may never change.

The suggestion of the numerous terraces on Blais's property is seen in this image of the peach tree orchard, photographed in late summer.

On a lower terrace, a serene contemporary addition by Blais is the pale gray swimming pool. Designed in collaboration with the Parisian architect Jean-François Bodin, the clean lines and thick surrounding edge transform the feature into an image of an Islamic watercourse. Recalling those geometric-shaped mosque fountains of pure proportions and simple form, the sheet of water mirrors the changing sky when viewed from the villa terrace above.

This once-forgotten garden has resurfaced again in an entirely new light. Gardens are never overnight creations, but rather nurtured after long moments of reflection. It is in that development and evolution that a garden's true beauty and pleasure appear.

After excavating the tangled growth that had run rampant for years, Blais discovered old yucca plants in a sloped bed. Rather than remove them he planted additional ones, flanked by flowering French lavender. Elsewhere on his Provence property, the artist incorporated existing exotic varieties, probably dating from the construction of the villa in the 1920s, with new plantings such as santolina or fruit trees.

A corner of a water tank sprouts a clump of aquatic irises. Blais removed the brambles that engulfed the feature and instead cultivated the untamed atmosphere with grasses and flowering Bonytip Fleabane or Mexican Daisy, Erigeron Karvinskianus, *gone to seed. Like many of the existing features that were discovered, the concrete pool was set with decorative motifs of inlaid pebbles.*

Overleaf: Inspired by the numerous concrete and pebble walks, water features, and steps that were unearthed during the restoration of the site, Blais created this terrace to one side of the villa. Alternating concrete pavers with insets of river-washed stones are laid in a checkerboard pattern with squares of grass. In the middle of the alluring feature, the artist planted a small lemon tree, which he hopes will survive the cool winter temperatures of the high elevation.

JENNIFER BARTLETT

NEW YORK / NEW YORK
1991

Opposite: Like a long reflecting pool, the low planter box, filled with alternating rows of blue-tinged fescue grasses, Festuca glauca *and* F. amethystina *'Superba', is the Grass Garden. It had been originally planned to contain a sea of lavender by Jennifer Bartlett who wanted to create the experience of windblown fields. Flanked on one side by dense columnar pillars of yew,* Taxus baccata *'Hatsfield', the garden is one of the five that compose the third-floor rooftop space.*

Heavy bowers of 'New Dawn' climbing rose frame the distant view and lead into the sunniest area of the entire garden complex. From giant clouds of Nepeta mussinii *'Blue Wonder' rises the collection of repeat-blooming roses separated by color with white 'Iceberg' in one bed, yellow and cream in another, and vivid scarlets and bright pinks in the third.*

Over the years a deep connection has been formed by Jennifer Bartlett between art and the landscape. As anyone who has observed her work knows, one of the dominating ideas is that of order set within the context of the garden. Elements such as grids and plaids, mathematical combinations, and such simple forms as a house or a tree or a boat take root in the natural, observed world. As seen in such works as the monumental 988-panel *Rhapsody* of 1975–76 or the suite of 197 drawings titled *In the Garden*, made in 1982, the garden in its infinite state of change is repeatedly explored.

Prelude to Jennifer Bartlett's city garden in New York was her rooftop garden in Paris and a plan to develop a garden in Manhattan's Battery Park City South Garden. Indeed, a strong factor in choosing to purchase a former railroad warehouse in Greenwich Village was the artist's desire to create a garden within an urban setting. It was at that point, in the late summer of 1989, that I met with Jennifer to begin plans for her garden.

The opportunity to collaborate with an artist is to enter into a very private and personal relationship. When an artist looks at a garden the first thing to go is convention—suddenly there are no rules, and this above all is one of the most liberating of experiences for a trained garden designer. The best gardens bear the mark of their creator, and when that person is someone like Jennifer Bartlett, the prospects for creating a design are wide open. Working with Jennifer Bartlett resulted in a garden that challenged me, and caused both of us to look very hard at possibilities that would express her strong feelings about design—about symmetry and order, color and texture. The result was a three-tiered garden with no less than twenty different varieties of garden themes.

The artist's garden site is a complex one, acutely wedged between surrounding neighboring brick facades and exposed to the city's harsh climatic changes. From the start, Bartlett's position was to create from the 16,000-square-foot structure a gardenscape that would be totally integrated with the interior living space. Unlike the severe street side of the building, which masks any impression of a garden, the back of the building resembles a stepped Assyrian ziggurat and progresses upward from the basement level to the highest elevation, in a vertical sequence of terraces. The four-story structure is divided into two working studio floors and two more for residential; for the exterior, this translates into three individual exterior spaces—one at ground level and two rooftop areas, the summit of which is defined by a 50-foot-long lap pool. Composed of glass walls, the rear facades invite direct interaction between both the interior and exterior spaces, and also reinforces the sequential effects. The very specific layout that governs the building design directly reflects Bartlett's own use of grids and geometrics in her paintings and sculptures.

Equally decisive in the garden's general formation and evolving from the artist's desire for a diversity of experiences was the concept of roomlike theme gardens, loosely inspired by Lawrence Johnston's Hidcote Manor in England, which Bartlett believes to be the twentieth-century's preeminent Western garden. Also dictated by the structure's existing roof loads was the layout for the two terraced gardens, including the placement of the galvanized planter boxes, which range from a mere nine inches in height to just under three feet. The intricate grid of plant containers transformed the two levels and created the idea of contained discovery and half-hidden views. Never at any one point are the three garden spaces entirely visible, which only increases the feeling of far greater scale and imbues the whole with a sense of intimacy.

The garden was formally instated May 1991. Unlike most landscape renovations or installations which are carried out over the course of seasons, Jennifer Bartlett's garden was entirely in place in just over three weeks: the intricate watering systems, the delivery and placement of 42 tons of topsoil, the hundreds of trees, shrubs, perennials, and annuals, and the more than 2,000 bulbs set on bricked pavers and in containers came into being.

The Shade Garden, set at the back of the property, has become a woodlands of soaring 26-foot-tall birch trees set on window axial alignments and underplanted with hollies,

Here on the second floor, a wall-mounted fountain trickles into an eighteen-foot-long trough, filled with Japanese koi fish and aquatic plants. The running water sonorously transforms the enclosure and masks the loud summer noises of rumbling air conditioners.

astilbes, ferns, wild ginger, and hostas. Late fall flowering cyclamen add notes of color and newly planted boxwood mounds will eventually be clipped into wavelike shapes.

In contrast, the second-level garden, just off the residential floor, has an open-air seating area flanked on either side by pairs of tall gnarled Japanese white pines, planted with prostrate junipers, dwarf spruce, and evergreen ivies. Ten-foot-high cream-painted cinderblock walls, with gridded appatures, were erected to screen neighboring views and are softened with trained wisteria, clematis, hydrangeas, and espaliered euonymus. Side beds are planted in large masses of single varieties. To the side a spiral staircase rises to the top level composed of five distinct garden areas: rose, grasses, heather, shrub, and the combined apple orchard and grapevine pergola.

Passing under metal hoops intertwined with Chinese wisteria, Baltic ivy, and roses, the brick path leads through the rose garden organized in layout by color. Adjoining the rose garden are the grapevine pergola, potting shed, and sod lawn. Four raised beds, each planted with wide branching crabapples, are individually planted with single varieties of *Alchemilla mollis, Geranium* × 'Johnson's Blue', *Sedum* 'Ruby Glow', and *Stachys byzantina.* The grass garden is guarded by square planters of columnar yew pillars or iron vine supports overplanted with honeysuckle, clematis, and morning glories. Edged by narrow brick paths is the

In the Shade Garden smooth river-washed white stones have been put at the bases of the clumped 'Whitespire' birch, which were chosen for their adaptability to the muggy summer months and for their striking chalky white verticals that provide interest in the winter. The dappled shade in the woodland is the only wind-protected area at Bartlett's and creates a peaceful place to sit.

heather garden, made up of a series of diagonally set beds. These are planted out with different varieties of heathers that bloom in succession from late August till early December.

The general symmetry of the garden is again emphasized with an ordered row of yew pillars, which balance the yews in the grass garden. These yews are engulfed in late spring with drifts of lavender weighed down by peonies, irises, and multicolored lupins. The shrub garden, a counterpart to the rose garden, is accessed by a short flight of brick steps that lead to a small circular mowed lawn ringed with an espaliered pear fence. Contained within is a teeming mass of plant materials, including blueberry and butterfly bushes, a single wisteria standard, and a miniature camellia collection. Although the underlying factor that governed plant selections was their hardiness in relation to New York's severe climate, many plants have fared surprisingly well, such as the roses, santolinas, and magnolias, while others have failed, such as euonymus and summer annuals like cosmos or flowering tobacco.

The sheer structure and amount of plants in this otherwise confined landscape is what make it both so unusual and undeniably awesome. In its brief two years it has taken on the characteristics of a Jennifer Bartlett painting, that provocative domain where order and life powerfully, wonderfully, fittingly belong together.

Viewed from above, the second-story garden is divided into rectangular beds edged in boxwood, Buxus sempervirens 'Newport Blue'. This area of the garden has undergone the most revision. In spring, the eight beds flower with different varieties of daffodils, while in summer the perennials become clouds of Russian sage, coreopsis, or Japanese anemones. Summer annuals such as marigolds and impatiens fill bare spots, while in winter the beds are mulched and covered with pine boughs.

Pages 202–3: A view of the diagonal grid garden on the third floor. Here the beds are protected with pine boughs for overwintering and the clay pots are wrapped in heavy burlap. Placed at the intersection of the brick paths are large clay pots, which are changed seasonally. For their winter display, fourteen different varieties of conifers are set out, while come spring the pots will be replaced with bright tulips and vivid pansies to be followed by cosmos in summer and dahlias in autumn.

Pages 204–5: To further increase the tension between the silvery blue-tinged fescue grasses, Bartlett planted a few clumps of Japanese blood grass, Imperata cyclindrica 'Red Baron'.

GARDENS OPEN TO
THE PUBLIC

VANESSA BELL AND DUNCAN GRANT
Charleston Farmhouse
near Firle
Lewes BN8 6LL
England
Tel. 44 0323 811265

GUSTAVE CAILLEBOTTE
Parc Caillebotte
6, rue de Concy
91330 Yerres
France
Tel. 33 69 48 72 05

JACQUES MAJORELLE
Le Jardin Majorelle
Marrakech
Morocco
Tel. 212 4 31 23

CARL MILLES
Milles Garden
Carl Milles Vag 2
181 34 Lidingö
Sweden
Tel. 46 8 731 5060

JOAN MIRÓ
Fondation Marguerite et Aime Maeght
06570 St.-Paul-de-Vence
France
Tel. 33 93 32 81 63

CLAUDE MONET
Fondation Claude Monet
Musée Claude Monet
27620 Giverny
France
Tel. 33 63 25 28 21

HENRY MOORE
The Henry Moore Foundation
Hertfordshire
England
Tel. 44 0279 84 3333

ISAMU NOGUCHI FOUNDATION
32–37 Vernon Boulevard
Long Island City, New York 11106
United States
Tel. 718 545 8842

PIERRE-AUGUSTE RENOIR
Musée Renoir, Les Collettes
19, chemin des Colettes
06800 Cagnes-sur-Mer
France
Tel. 33 93 20 61 07

HUBERT ROBERT
Château de Versailles
78000 Versailles
France
Tel. 33 30 84 74 00

PETER PAUL RUBENS
Rubenshuis
Wapper 9–11
2000 Antwerp
Belgium
Tel. 32 3 232 47 51

AUGUSTUS SAINT-GAUDENS
Saint-Gaudens National Historic Site
Cornish, New Hampshire
United States
Tel. 603 675 2175

JOAQUIN SOROLLA
Museo Sorolla
General Martinez Campos 37
Madrid 28010
Spain
Tel. 34 1 4101584

HIROSHI TESHIGAHARA
Sogetsu School
2–21 Akasaka 7 Chome
Minato-ku 107 Tokyo
Japan
Tel. 3 3408 1126

Favorite Fairy Tales
TOLD IN IRELAND

Favorite Fairy Tales

TOLD IN IRELAND

Retold from Irish Storytellers by

VIRGINIA HAVILAND

Illustrated by

ARTUR MAROKVIA

Boston　　LITTLE, BROWN AND COMPANY　　Toronto

These stories have been adapted from the following sources:

By permission of Mrs. Seumas MacManus:

THE BEE, THE HARP, THE MOUSE, AND THE BUM-CLOCK and THE OLD
HAG'S LONG LEATHER BAG, from DONEGAL FAIRY STORIES by Seumas
MacManus (Garden City, New York: Doubleday, Page and Com-
pany, 1900).

BILLY BEG AND THE BULL, from IN CHIMNEY CORNERS, by Seumas
MacManus (Garden City, New York: Doubleday, Page and Company, 1899).

By permission of Ruth Sawyer Durand:

THE WIDOW'S LAZY DAUGHTER, as told to Ruth Sawyer "under a lazy
bush in Donegal by a wandering tinker" (hitherto unpublished).

PATRICK O'DONNELL AND THE LEPRECHAUN, as told to Ruth Sawyer
by Patrick O'Donnell's great-granddaughter Dorothy Donelly
(hitherto unpublished).

Published simultaneously in Canada
by Little, Brown & Company (Canada) Limited

PRINTED IN THE UNITED STATES OF AMERICA

Contents

Retold by
Virginia Haviland

Favorite Fairy Tales
TOLD IN ENGLAND

Favorite Fairy Tales
TOLD IN GERMANY

Favorite Fairy Tales
TOLD IN FRANCE

Favorite Fairy Tales
TOLD IN NORWAY

Favorite Fairy Tales
TOLD IN IRELAND

Favorite Fairy Tales
TOLD IN RUSSIA

The Bee, the Harp, the Mouse, and the Bum-clock

ONCE A WIDOW had one son, called Jack. Jack and his mother owned just three cows. They lived well and were happy for a long time, but at last hard times came down on them. Their crops failed, and poverty looked in at the door. Indeed, things got so bad for the widow she had to make up her mind to sell one of their three cows.

"Jack," she said one night, "in the morning you must go to the fair to sell the branny cow."

In the morning brave Jack was up early. He took a stick in his fist and turned out the cow, and off he went with her.

When Jack came to the fair, he saw a great crowd gathered in a ring in the street. He went into the crowd to see what they were looking at. There in the middle of them he saw a man with a wee, wee harp, a mouse, and a cockroach, which is called a bum-clock, and a bee to play on the harp.

When the man put them down on the ground and whistled, the bee began to play the harp. The mouse and the bum-clock stood up on their hind legs and got hold of each other and began to waltz. And as soon as the harp began to play and the mouse and the bum-clock to dance, there wasn't a man or woman, or a thing in the fair, that didn't begin to dance also. The pots and pans, and the wheels and reels jumped and jigged all over the town, and Jack himself and the branny cow as much as the next. There was never a town in such a state before or since.

After a while the man picked up the bee, the harp, the mouse, and the bum-clock and put them into his pocket. The men and women, Jack and the cow, the pots and pans, the wheels and reels that had hopped and jigged now stopped, and every one began to laugh as if to break his heart.

The man turned to Jack. "Jack," said he, "how would you like to be master of all these animals?"

"Why," said Jack, "I should like it fine."

"Well, then," said the man, "how will we make a bargain about them?"

"I have no money," said Jack.

"But you have a fine cow," said the man. "I will give you the bee and the harp for it."

"Oh, but," Jack said, said he, "my poor mother at home is very sad entirely. I have this cow to sell and lift her heart again."

"And better than this she cannot get," said the man. "For when she sees the bee play the harp, she will laugh if she never laughed in her life before."

"Well," said Jack, said he, "that will be grand."

He made the bargain. The man took the cow, and Jack started home with the bee and the harp in his pocket. When he came home, his mother welcomed him back.

"And Jack," said she, "I see you have sold the cow."

"I have done that," said Jack.

"Did you do well?" said the mother.

"I did well, and very well," said Jack.

"How much did you get for her?" said the mother.

"Oh," said he, "it was not for money at all I sold her, but for something far better."

"Oh, Jack! Jack!" said she. "What have you done?"

"Just wait until you see, Mother," said he, "and you will soon say I have done well."

Out of his pocket he took the bee and the harp and set them in the middle of the floor, and whistled to them. As soon as he did this the bee began to play the harp. The mother she looked at them and let a big, great laugh out of her, and she and Jack began dancing and jigging. The pots and

pans, the wheels and reels also began to dance
and jig over the floor. And the house itself hopped
about, too.

When Jack picked up the bee and the harp
again, the dancing all stopped, and his mother she
laughed for a long time. But when she came to
herself, she got very angry entirely with Jack,
and she told him he was a silly, foolish fellow.
There was neither food nor money in the house,
and now he had lost one of her good cows, also.

"We must do something to live," said she.
"Over to the fair you must go tomorrow morning and take the black cow with you and sell her."

Off in the morning at an early hour brave Jack started, and never halted until he was in the fair.

When he came into the fair, he saw a big crowd gathered in a ring in the street. Said Jack to himself, "I wonder what they are looking at." Into the crowd he pushed, and saw the wee man this day again with a mouse and a bum-clock.

When the man put them down in the street and whistled, the mouse and the bum-clock stood up on their hind legs and got hold of each other. They began to dance there and jig. As they did, there was not a man or woman in the street who didn't begin to jig also. Jack and the black cow, the wheels and the reels, and the pots and pans— all of them were jigging and dancing all over the town. And the houses themselves were jumping and hopping about, too. Such a place Jack or anyone else never saw before.

When the man lifted the mouse and the bum-clock into his pocket, they all stopped dancing and settled down.

The man turned to Jack. "Jack," said he, "I am glad to see you. How would you like to have these animals?"

"I should like well to have them," said Jack, said he, "only I cannot."

"Why cannot you?" asked the man.

"Oh," said Jack, said he, "I have no money, and my poor mother is very downhearted. She sent me to the fair to sell this cow and bring some money to lift her heart."

"Oh," said the man, said he, "if you want to lift your mother's heart, I will sell you the mouse. When you set the bee to play the harp and the mouse to dance to it, your mother will laugh if she never laughed in her life before."

"But I have no money," said Jack, said he, "to buy your mouse."

"I don't mind," said the man, said he, "I will take your cow for it."

Poor Jack was so taken with the mouse and had his mind so set on it, that he thought it was

a grand bargain entirely. He gave the man his cow, and took the mouse and started off for home. When he got home his mother welcomed him.

"Jack," said she, "I see you have sold the cow."

"I did that," said Jack.

"Did you sell her well?" asked she.

"Very well indeed," said Jack, said he.

"How much did you get for her?"

"I didn't get money," said he, "but something far better."

"Oh, Jack! Jack!" said she. "What do you mean?"

"I will soon show you that, Mother," said he, taking the mouse out of his pocket, and the harp and the bee, and setting them all on the floor. When he began to whistle, the bee began to play, and the mouse got up on its hind legs and began to dance and jig. The mother gave such a hearty laugh as she never laughed in her life before. And she and Jack began dancing and jigging. The pots and pans and wheels and reels also began to dance and jig over the floor. And the house itself hopped all about, too.

When they were tired of this, Jack lifted the harp and the mouse and the bee and put them in his pocket, and his mother she laughed for a long time.

But when she came to herself, she got very angry entirely with Jack.

"Oh, Jack!" she said, "you are a stupid, good-for-nothing fellow. We have neither money nor meat in the house, and here you have lost two of my good cows, and I have only one left now. Tomorrow morning," she said, "you must be up early and take this cow to the fair and sell her. See you get something this time to lift my heart up."

"I will do that," said Jack, said he. And so he went to his bed.

Early in the morning Jack was up and turned out the spotty cow, and went again to the fair.

When Jack came into the fair, he saw a crowd gathered in a ring in the street. "I wonder what they are looking at, anyhow," said he. He pushed through the crowd, and there he saw the same wee man he had seen before, with a bum-clock.

When the man put the bum-clock on the ground, he whistled, and the bum-clock began to dance. And as soon as the bum-clock began to dance, the men, women and children in the street, and Jack and the spotty cow began to dance and jig also. Everything on the street and about it, the wheels and reels, the pots and pans, began to jig. And the houses themselves began to dance likewise.

When the man lifted the bum-clock and put it in his pocket, everybody stopped jigging and dancing and laughed loud. The wee man turned, and saw Jack.

"Jack, my brave boy," said he, "you will never be right-fixed until you have this bum-clock, for it is a very fancy thing to have."

"Oh, but," said Jack, said he, "I have no money."

"No matter for that," said the man, "you have a cow, and that is as good as money to me."

"Well," said Jack, "I have a poor mother who is very downhearted at home. She sent me to the fair to sell this cow and raise some money and lift her heart."

"Oh, but Jack," said the wee man, "this bum-clock is the very thing to lift her heart. When

you put down your harp and bee and mouse on
the floor, and put the bum-clock along with
them, she will laugh if she never laughed in her
life before."

"Well, that is surely true," said Jack, said he,
"and I think I will make a swap with you."

So Jack gave the cow to the man, and took
the bum-clock himself, and started for home. His
mother was glad to see Jack back.

"And Jack," said she, "I see that you have sold
the cow."

"I did that, Mother."

"Did you sell her well, Jack?" said his mother.

"Very well indeed, Mother," said Jack.

"How much did you get for her?" said his·
mother.

"I didn't take any money for her, Mother, but
something far better," said Jack. He took out of
his pocket the bum-clock and the mouse, and the
bee and the harp, and set them on the floor and
began to whistle. The bee began to play the harp,
and the mouse and the bum-clock stood up on
their hind legs and began to dance, and Jack's
mother laughed very hearty. Everything in the
house, the wheels and the reels and the pots and
pans, went jigging and hopping over the floor.
And the house itself went jigging and hopping
about likewise.

When Jack lifted up the animals and put them
in his pocket, everything stopped, and the mother
laughed for a good while. But after a bit, when
she came to herself, she saw what Jack had done

and how they were without money, or food, or a cow. She got very, very angry at Jack. She scolded him hard, and then sat down and began to cry.

Poor Jack, when he looked at himself, confessed that he was a stupid fool entirely.

"And what," said he, "shall I now do for my poor mother?"

One day soon, Jack went out along the road, thinking and thinking, and he met a wee woman who said, "Good morrow to you, Jack. How is it you are not trying for the daughter of the King of Ireland?"

"What do you mean?" said Jack.

Said she, "Didn't you hear what the whole world has heard, that the King of Ireland has a daughter who hasn't laughed for seven years? He has promised to give her in marriage, and to give the kingdom along with her, to any man who will take three laughs out of her."

"If that is so," said Jack, said he, "it is not here I should be."

Back to the house he went, and gathered together the bee, the harp, the mouse, and the bum-clock. Putting them into his pocket, he bade his mother good-by. He told her it wouldn't be long till she got good news from him, and off he hurried.

When Jack reached the castle, there was a ring of spikes all round and men's heads on nearly every spike there.

"What heads are these?" Jack asked one of the
King's soldiers.

"Any man that comes here trying to win the King's daughter, and fails to make her laugh three times, he loses his head and has it stuck on a spike. These are the heads of the men that failed," said he.

"A mighty big crowd," said Jack, said he. Then Jack sent word to tell the King's daughter and the King that there was a new man who had come to win her.

In a very little time the King and the King's daughter and the King's Court all came out. They sat themselves down on gold and silver chairs in front of the castle, and ordered Jack to be brought in until he should have his trial.

Jack, before he went, took out of his pocket the bee, the harp, the mouse, and the bum-clock. He gave the harp to the bee, and he tied a string to one and the other. He took the end of the string himself, and marched into the castle yard before all the Court, with his animals coming on a string behind him.

When the Queen and the King and the Court saw poor ragged Jack with his bee, his mouse, and with his bum-clock hopping behind him on a string, they set up one roar of laughter that was long and loud enough. And when the King's daughter herself lifted her head to

see what they were laughing at, and saw Jack
and his menagerie, she opened her mouth and she
let out of her such a laugh as was never heard
before.

Jack made a low bow, and said, "Thank you,
my lady. You have given me one of the three
laughs."

Then he drew up his animals in a circle, and
began to whistle. The minute he did so, the bee
began to play the harp. The mouse and the bum-
clock stood up on their hind legs, got hold of
each other, and began to dance. The King and
the King's Court and Jack himself began to dance
and jig, and everything about the King's castle—
pots and pans, wheels and reels—and the castle
itself began to dance also. And the King's daughter, when she saw this, opened her mouth again.
She let out of her a laugh twice louder than she
let before.

Jack, in the middle of his jigging, made another bow, and said, "Thank you, my lady. You have given me two of the three laughs."

Jack and his animals went on playing and dancing. But Jack could not get the third laugh out of the King's daughter, and the poor lad saw his big head in danger of going on the spike.

Then the brave mouse came to Jack's help and

wheeled around upon its heel. As it did so, its tail swiped into the bum-clock's mouth, and the bum-clock began to cough and cough and cough.

When the King's daughter saw this, she opened her mouth again, and she let out the loudest and hardest and merriest laugh that was ever heard before or since.

"Thank you, my lady," said Jack, making another bow. "I have all of you won."

When Jack stopped his animals, the King took him and the animals within the castle. Jack was washed and combed. He was dressed in a suit of silk and satin, with all kinds of gold and silver ornaments, and then was led before the King's daughter. And true enough, she confessed that a handsomer and finer fellow than Jack she had never seen. She was very willing to be his wife.

Jack sent for his poor old mother and brought her to the wedding, which lasted nine days and nine nights, and every night was better than the other.

The Old Hag's Long Leather Bag

ONCE UPON A TIME, long, long ago, a widow woman had three daughters. When their father died, their mother thought they would never be in want, for he had left her a long leather bag filled with gold and silver. But he was not long dead, when an old hag came begging one day and stole the long leather bag filled with gold and silver. She went out of the country with it, no one knew where.

From that day, the widow woman had a hard struggle to bring up her three daughters.

When they were grown, the eldest said one day, "Mother, I'm a young woman now, and it's a shame for me to be here doing nothing to help you or myself. Bake me a bannock and I'll go away to push my fortune."

The mother baked her a bannock, and asked would she have half of it with her blessing or the whole of it without. The girl answered that she would take the whole without the blessing.

Off she went, after saying that if she was not back in a year and a day, they would know she was doing well, and making her fortune.

She traveled away and away, farther than I could tell you, and twice as far as you could tell me, until she came into a strange country.

Going up to a little house, the girl found an old hag living in it. When the hag asked her where she was going, she said, "I'm on my way to push my fortune."

"How would you like to stay here with me?" asked the hag. "I'm needing a maid myself."

"What will I have to do?"

"You will have to wash me and dress me, and sweep the hearth clean. But on the peril of your life, do you never look up the chimney," answered the hag.

"All right," she agreed.

The next day, when the hag arose, the girl washed her and dressed her, and when the hag went out, she swept the hearth clean. But she thought it would do no harm to have one wee look up the chimney. And what did she see but her own mother's long leather bag of gold and silver! She took it down at once, and, getting it on her back, started away for home as fast as she could run.

She had not gone far when she met a horse grazing in a field. When he saw her, he called out, "Rub me! Rub me! I haven't been rubbed these seven years."

But she only struck him with a stick and drove him out of her way.

She had not gone much farther when she met a sheep. "Oh, shear me! Shear me!" begged the sheep. "I haven't been shorn these seven years."

But she struck the sheep, and sent it scurrying out of her way.

She had not gone much farther when she met a goat. "Oh, change my tether! Change my tether!" cried the goat. "It hasn't been changed these seven years."

But she flung a stone at him, and went on.

Next she came to a mill. The mill cried out, "Oh, turn me! Turn me! I haven't been turned these seven years."

But she did not heed what it said. She only went in and lay down behind the mill door, with the bag under her head, for it was then night.

When the hag came into her hut again, she saw that the girl was gone. Over to the chimney she ran, to see if she had carried off the bag. In a great rage because it was missing, she started to run as fast as she could after her.

She had not gone far when she met the horse, and asked, "Oh, horse, horse of mine, did you see this maid of mine, with my tig, with my tag, with my long leather bag, and all the gold and silver I have earned since I was a maid?"

"Ay," said the horse, "it is not long since she passed here."

The hag ran on and on, until she met the sheep. "Sheep, sheep of mine, did you see this maid of mine, with my tig, with my tag, with my long leather bag, and all the gold and silver I have earned since I was a maid?"

"Ay," said the sheep, "it is not long since she passed here."

So she went on and on, until she met the goat. "Goat, goat of mine, did you see this maid of mine, with my tig, with my tag, with my long leather bag, and all the gold and silver I have earned since I was a maid?"

"Ay," said the goat, "it is not long since she passed here."

The hag went on farther, until she met the mill. "Mill, mill of mine, did you see this maid of mine, with my tig, with my tag, with my

long leather bag, and all the gold and silver I have earned since I was a maid?"

And the mill answered, "Yes, she is sleeping behind the door."

The hag went in and struck the girl with a white rod, which turned her into a stone. She then lifted the bag of gold and silver onto her back, and went away home.

A year and a day went by after the eldest daughter left home. Since she had not returned, the second daughter now spoke up. "My sister must be doing well and making her fortune. Isn't it a shame for me to be sitting here doing nothing, either to help you, Mother, or myself? Bake me a bannock and I'll go away to push my fortune."

The mother did this, and asked her if she would have half the bannock with her blessing or the whole bannock without.

The girl answered that she would take the whole bannock without the blessing. As she went off she added, "If I am not back here in a year and a day, you may be sure that I am doing well and making my fortune."

She traveled away and away, farther than I could tell you, and twice as far as you could tell me, until she came into a strange country.

There, now, with this second daughter, all happened as it had before with the eldest. She too was struck with the hag's white rod and turned into a stone. And the hag lifted the bag of gold and silver onto her back, and went away home once more.

When the second daughter had been gone a year and a day, the youngest daughter said, "My two sisters must be doing very well indeed, and making great fortunes. It's a shame for me to be sitting here doing nothing, either to help you, Mother, or myself. Make me a bannock and I will go away and push my fortune."

The mother did this, and asked her if she would have half of the bannock with her blessing or the whole bannock without.

The girl answered, "I will have half of the bannock with your blessing, Mother."

The mother gave her a blessing and half a bannock, and off she went.

She traveled away and away, farther than I could tell you and twice as far as you could tell me, until she came to a strange country.

Going up to a little house, this daughter, too, met the old hag, and agreed to work as her maid.

All went the same with her as with her two sisters, until she began running away with the long leather bag of gold and silver.

When she got to the horse, the horse called out, "Rub me! Rub me! For I haven't been rubbed these seven years."

"Oh, poor horse, poor horse," the kind youngest daughter said at once. "I'll surely do that." She laid down her bag, and rubbed the horse.

Then she went on, and it wasn't long before she met the sheep. "Oh, shear me, shear me!" begged the sheep. "I haven't been shorn these seven years."

"Oh, poor sheep, poor sheep," she answered. "I'll surely do that." She laid down the bag, and sheared the sheep.

On she went till she met the goat. "Oh, change my tether! Change my tether!" cried the goat. "It hasn't been changed these seven years."

"Oh, poor goat, poor goat," she said. "I'll surely do that."

She laid down the bag, and changed the goat's tether.

At last she reached the mill. "Oh, turn me!

Turn me!" cried the mill. "I haven't been turned these seven years."

"Oh, poor mill, poor mill," she replied. "I'll surely do that." And she turned the mill.

As night was on her now, she went in and lay down behind the mill door to sleep.

When the hag came into her hut again, she found the girl gone. Over to the chimney she ran, to see if she had carried off the bag. In a great rage because it was missing, she started to run as fast as she could after her.

She had not gone far when she met the horse and asked, "Oh, horse, horse of mine, did you see this maid of mine, with my tig, with my tag, with my long leather bag, and all the gold and silver I have earned since I was a maid?"

The horse answered, "Do you think I have nothing to do but watch your maids for you? You may go somewhere else and look."

She went on and soon came upon the sheep. "Oh, sheep, sheep of mine, have you seen this maid of mine, with my tig, with my tag, with my long leather bag, and all the gold and silver I have earned since I was a maid?"

The sheep said, "Do you think I have nothing to do but watch your maids for you? You may go somewhere else and look."

She went on till she met the goat. "Oh, goat, goat of mine, have you seen this maid of mine, with my tig, with my tag, with my long leather bag, and all the gold and silver I have earned since I was a maid?"

The goat said, "Do you think I have nothing to do but watch your maids for you? You can go somewhere else and look."

At last she came to the mill. "Oh, mill, mill of mine, have you seen this maid of mine, with my tig, with my tag, with my long leather bag, and all the gold and silver I have earned since I was a maid?"

The mill said, "Come nearer and whisper to me."

The hag went nearer to whisper to the mill—but the mill dragged her under the wheels and ground her up.

The old hag had dropped the white rod. The mill told the girl to take it and strike two stones behind the mill door. As soon as she did this, up sprang her two sisters, ready to go home. The youngest one lifted the leather bag onto her back, and the three of them traveled away and away until they reached their own land.

Their mother, who had been crying all the time they were away, was now overjoyed to see them. And rich and happy they all lived ever after.

Billy Beg and the Bull

ONCE ON A TIME when pigs were swine, a King and a Queen had one son and he was called Billy Beg. Now the Queen gave Billy a bull that he was very fond of, and it was just as fond of him. But after some time the Queen died. Her last request to the King had been that he would never part Billy and his bull, and the King promised that come what might, come what may, he would not.

Soon the King married again. The new Queen didn't take to Billy Beg, and no more did she like the bull, seeing himself and Billy so friendly. No way could she get the King to part Billy and the bull, so she asked a henwife what she could do.

"And what will you give me," asked the henwife, "if I very soon part them?"

"Whatever you ask," said the Queen.

"Well and good then," said the henwife. "You

are to take to your bed. You must pretend that you are bad with a complaint, and I'll do the rest of it."

The Queen took to her bed and none of the doctors could do anything for her. So the Queen asked for the henwife. When she came and examined the Queen, she said there was one thing, and only one, could cure her.

The King asked what was that. The henwife said it was three mouthfuls of the blood of Billy Beg's bull. But the King wouldn't hear of this.

The next day the Queen was worse. The third day she was worse still. She told the King she was dying, and he'd have her death on his head. So, at last, the King had to consent to the killing of Billy Beg's bull.

When Billy heard this he got very down in the heart entirely. The bull saw him looking so mournful, and asked what was wrong with him. So Billy told the bull what was wrong. The bull told him never to mind, but to keep up his heart.

The Queen would never taste a drop of his blood.

The next day, when the bull was led up to be killed, said he to Billy, "Jump up on my back till we see what kind of a horseman you are."

Up Billy jumped on his back. With that the bull leaped nine miles high, nine miles deep, and nine miles broad, and came down with Billy sticking between his horns.

Hundreds were looking on dazed at the sight, and through them the bull rushed, right over the Queen, killing her dead.

Away the bull galloped, over high hills and low, over the Cove of Cork and old Tom Fox with his bugle horn.

At last they stopped. "Now then," said the bull to Billy, "put your hand in my left ear, and you'll find a napkin. When you spread it out, it will be covered with food and drink of all sorts, fit for the King himself."

Billy did this, and then he spread out the napkin. He ate and drank to his heart's content, then he rolled the napkin and put it back in the bull's ear.

"And now," said the bull, "put your hand into my right ear and you'll find a bit of a stick. If you wind it over your head three times, it will turn into a sword and give you the strength of a thousand men besides your own. When you have no more need of it as a sword, it will change back into a stick again."

Billy did all this. "Well and good," said the bull. "At twelve o'clock tomorrow I'll have to meet and fight a great bull."

Billy got up again on the bull's back. The bull started off and away, over high hills and low, over the Cove of Cork and old Tom Fox with his bugle horn.

There they stopped and Billy's bull met the other bull. Both of them fought, and the like of their fight was never seen before or since. They knocked the soft ground into hard, and the hard into soft, the soft into spring wells, the spring wells into rocks, and the rocks into high hills. They fought long, and Billy Beg's bull killed the other, and drank his blood.

Billy took the napkin out of the bull's ear

again. He spread it out and ate a hearty dinner.

Then said the bull to Billy, said he, "At twelve o'clock tomorrow, I'm to meet the brother of the bull I killed today, and we'll have a hard fight."

Billy got on the bull's back again, and the bull started off, over high hills and low, over the Cove of Cork and old Tom Fox with his bugle horn.

Here he met the bull's brother, and they set to and fought long and hard. At last Billy's bull killed the other and drank his blood.

Again, Billy took the napkin out of the bull's ear and spread it out and ate a hearty dinner.

Now said the bull to Billy, said he, "Tomorrow at twelve o'clock I'm to fight the brother of the two bulls I killed. He's a mighty bull entirely, the strongest of them all. He's called the Black Bull of the Forest, and he'll be too much for me.

"When I'm dead," said the bull, "you, Billy, will take with you the napkin, and you'll never be hungry; and the stick, and you'll be able to overcome everything that gets in your way. And take out your knife and cut a strip off my hide, and make a belt of it. As long as you wear this belt, you cannot be killed."

Billy was very sorry to hear this. But he got up on the bull's back again, and they started off.

Sure enough, at twelve o'clock the next day they met the great Black Bull of the Forest. Both of the bulls began to fight, and they fought hard and long. But at last the Black Bull of the Forest killed Billy Beg's bull, and drank his blood.

Billy Beg was so sad at this that for two days he sat over the bull. He neither ate nor drank, but cried salt tears all the time.

After the two days, Billy got up. He spread out the napkin and ate a hearty dinner, for he was very hungry now. Then he cut a strip off the hide of the bull and made a belt for himself. Taking it and the bit of stick, and the napkin, he set out to push his fortune.

Well now, Billy traveled for three days and

three nights until at last he came to a great gentleman's place. He asked the gentleman if he
could give him work, and the man said he wanted
just such a boy as him for herding cattle.

Billy asked what cattle would he have to herd,
and what wages would he get.

The gentleman said he had three goats, three
cows, three horses, and three donkeys that he fed
in an orchard. Also, he said that no boy who went
with them ever came back alive, for there were
three giants—and these were brothers—that came
to milk the cows and the goats every day. Always

they killed the boy that was herding. If Billy wished to try, he could, but they wouldn't fix his wages until they'd see if he would come back alive.

"Agreed, then," said Billy.

The next morning Billy got up and drove the animals to the orchard and began to feed them. About the middle of the day he heard three terrible roars that shook the apples off the trees, shook the horns on the cows, and made the hair stand up on Billy's head.

In came a frightful big giant with three heads, and began to threaten Billy. "You're too big for one bite, and too small for two," bellowed the giant. "What will I do with you?"

"I'll fight you," answered Billy, stepping out to him and swinging the bit of stick three times over his head. The stick changed into a sword and gave him the strength of a thousand men besides his own.

But the giant laughed at the size of him. "Well, how will I kill you?" asked he. "Will it be by a swing by the back or a cut of the sword?"

"With a swing by the back," said Billy, "if you can."

They both laid hold for a wrestle, and Billy lifted the giant clean off the ground.

"Oh, have mercy," said the giant. But Billy took up his sword and killed the giant then and there.

It was evening by this time, so Billy drove home the three goats, three cows, three horses, and three donkeys. That night all the dishes in the house could not hold the milk the cows had to give.

"Well," said the gentleman, "this beats me. I

never saw anyone coming back alive out of there before, nor the cows with a drop of milk. Did you see anything in the orchard?" asked he.

"Nothing worse than myself," said Billy. "And what about my wages now?"

"Well," said the gentleman, "you'll hardly come alive out of the orchard tomorrow. So we'll wait until after that."

Next morning his master told Billy that something must have happened to one of the giants. He used to hear the cries of three giants every night, but last night he only heard two crying.

That morning, after Billy had eaten breakfast, he drove the animals into the orchard again, and began to feed them.

About twelve o'clock he heard three terrible roars that shook the apples off the trees, the horns on the cows, and made the hair stand up on Billy's head. In came a frightful big giant, with six heads. He told Billy he would make him pay for killing his brother yesterday. "You're too big for one bite, and too small for two. What will I do with you?" bellowed the giant.

Well, the long and the short of it is that Billy lifted this giant clean off the ground, too, and took up his sword and killed him then and there.

It was evening by this time, so Billy drove the animals home again. The milk the cows gave that night overflowed all the dishes in the house, and, running out, turned a rusty mill that hadn't been turned for thirty years.

If the master was surprised to see Billy come back the night before, he was ten times more sur-

prised now. "Did you see anything in the orchard today?"

"Nothing worse than myself," said Billy. "And what about my wages now?"

"Well, never mind about your wages till to-morrow," said the gentleman. "I think you'll hardly come back alive again."

Billy went to his bed, and the gentleman went to his.

When the gentleman rose in the morning, said he to Billy, "I don't know what's wrong with two of the giants. Only one did I hear crying last night."

Well, when Billy had eaten his breakfast, he set out to the orchard once more, driving before him the animals.

Sure enough, about the middle of the day he heard three terrible roars again. In came another giant, this one with twelve heads on him.

"You villain, you," thundered the giant. "You killed my two brothers, and I'll have my revenge on you now. But you're too big for one bite, and too small for two. What will I do with you?"

Again it ended with brave Billy lifting the giant clean off the ground, and taking his sword, and killing him.

That evening Billy drove his animals home. This time the milk of the cows had to be turned into a valley, where it made a lake three miles long, and three miles broad, and three miles deep.

Now the gentleman wondered more than ever to find Billy back alive. "Did you see nothing in the orchard today, Billy?" he asked.

"No, nothing worse than myself," said Billy.

"Well, that beats me," said the gentleman.

"What about my wages now?" asked Billy.

"Well, you're a good mindful boy," said the gentleman, "and I'll give you any wages you ask for the future."

The next morning the gentleman said to Billy, "Not one giant did I hear crying last night. I don't know what has happened to them."

That day the gentleman said to Billy, "Now you must look after the cattle again, Billy, while I go to see the fight."

"What fight?" asked Billy.

"Why," said the gentleman, "the King's daughter is going to be eaten by a fiery dragon, if the greatest fighter in the land doesn't kill the dragon first. And if he's able to kill the dragon, the King is to give him his daughter in marriage."

"That will be fine," said Billy.

Billy drove the animals to the orchard again, and the like of all the people that passed by that day to see the fight he had never seen before. They went in coaches and carriages, on horses and donkeys, riding and walking, crawling and creeping. Said one man that was passing, to Billy, "Why don't you come to see the great fight?"

"What would take the likes of me there?" said Billy.

But when Billy found them all gone, he saddled and bridled the best black horse his master had.

He put on the best suit of clothes he could get in his master's house, and rode off to the fight after the rest.

When he arrived, he saw the King's daughter with the whole court about her on a platform before the castle. He had never before seen anything half so beautiful.

The great warrior that was to fight the dragon was walking up and down on the lawn before her, with three men carrying his sword. And everyone in the whole country was gathered there looking at him.

But when the fiery dragon came up, with twelve heads on him and every mouth spitting fire, and let twelve roars out of him, the warrior ran away and hid himself up to the neck in a well of water. No one could get him to come and face the dragon.

The King's daughter asked then if there was no one there to save her from the dragon. But no one stirred.

When Billy saw this, he tied the belt of the bull's hide around him, swung his stick over his head, and went in.

After a terrible fight entirely, he killed the dragon. And then everyone gathered about to find out who the stranger was. But Billy jumped on his horse and darted away sooner than let them know. Only, just as he was getting away, the King's daughter pulled the shoe off his foot.

Now when the dragon was killed, the warrior that had hid in the well came out. He brought the dragon's heads to the King, and said that it was he in disguise who had killed the dragon.

But the King's daughter tried the shoe on him and found it didn't fit. And she said she would marry no one but the man the shoe fitted.

When Billy got home he quickly took off the fine suit, and he had the horse in the stable and the cattle all home before his master returned.

When the master came, he began telling Billy about the wonderful day they had had entirely. He told about the grand stranger that came riding down out of a cloud on a black horse, and killed the fiery dragon, and then vanished in a cloud again.

"Now, Billy," said he, "wasn't that wonderful?"

"It was, indeed," said Billy, "very wonderful entirely."

After that it was announced over the country that all the people were to come to the King's castle on a certain day, so that the King's daughter could try the shoe on them. The one it fitted, she was to marry.

When the day arrived, Billy was in the orchard with the three goats, three cows, three horses, and three donkeys, as usual.

The like of all the crowds that passed that day

going to the King's castle to try on the shoe, he had never seen before. They all asked Billy if he was not going to the King's castle, but Billy said, "Now, what would be bringing the likes of me there?"

At last when all the others had gone, there passed an old man wearing a scarecrow suit of

rags. Billy stopped him and asked what he would take to swap clothes with him.

"Now don't be playing off your jokes on my clothes," said the old man, "or maybe I'll be making you feel my stick."

But Billy soon let him see it was in earnest he was, and both of them swapped suits. Billy, however, did not give up his belt.

Off to the castle started Billy, with the suit of rags on his back and an old stick in his hand. When he got there, he found everyone in great commotion trying on the shoe. Some of them were cutting down a foot, trying to get it to fit. But it was all of no use: the shoe would fit none.

The King's daughter was about to give up in despair when a ragged-looking boy, which was Billy, elbowed his way through, and asked, "Let me try it on; maybe it would fit me."

But the people all began to laugh at the sight of him. "Go along," said they, shoving and pushing him back.

But the King's daughter saw him, and called out to let him come and try on the shoe.

So Billy went up, and all the people looked on, breaking their hearts with laughing. But what would you have of it—the shoe fitted Billy as nice as if it was made on his foot! And so the King's daughter claimed Billy as her husband. He confessed it was he that had killed the fiery dragon.

When the King had Billy dressed up in a silk and satin suit, with plenty of gold and silver on it, everyone gave in that his like they had never seen before.

Billy was married to the King's daughter, and the wedding listed nine days, nine hours, nine minutes, nine half minutes, and nine quarter minutes; and they lived happy and well from that day to this.

The Widow's Lazy Daughter

LONG AGO there lived in Donegal a poor widow. She had one daughter, the prettiest and the laziest girl in the whole of Ireland. Not a stroke of work would she put her hand to—not from cockcrow to candletime. The poor widow worked the lee-long day to keep the cabin tidy and gather in enough food to feed the two of them.

At last the widow lost heart entirely. Leaving early one morning to do a half-day's work for a neighbor, she said to the girl, "Today you'll be doing your share of the work. You'll clean the cabin proper and make the stirabout. You'll be taking care not to burn it, for it's the last meal we have in the chest. If you burn it, the two of us will go hungry the day."

With that she was off. The girl, Eileen, watching her go, sent a great sighing after her. "Work!"

said she, and she sniffed. " 'Tis little liking I have for it. The longer I can put off the cleaning of the cabin the better. I'll make first the stirabout."

She built up the turf on the fire and filled up the pot with water. She hung it over the turf and stirred in the meal. Then she fetched the creepy-stool close to the hearth and sat down. With a lazy hand she began to stir, lest the meal stick to the pot and burn there. She stirred once, she stirred twice, she stirred three times. Then her hand fell to her lap and she began her dreaming.

It was always the same dream—a life with no work to it; a castle to live in, mayhap; and who but the King of Ireland's son to make her his bride!

I cannot be telling you how long she dreamed; but I can tell you what fetched her out of the dreaming—a burst of smoke from the pot where the stirabout had burned to fine blackness. With the smoke came a fearsome smell. Eileen was off the stool to the door to fling it wide. And what

did she find on the step, outside, waiting to be let in, but the poor widow herself. She saw the smoke and she smelled the smell. For the first time in her life she raised her hand against the girl, "Lass, lass,

the time has come to be beating the laziness out of you." And with that she took up a stick of blackthorn and clouted the girl, out the door, down the road to the crossroads.

And who should be riding by but the King of Ireland's son, himself! He was a handsome lad and his clothes were the finest. He rode a great white horse with a red-and-gold saddlecloth and wee small golden bells on the bridle to ring his coming. He stopped, looking first at the girl and then at the widow. " 'Tis a shameful thing," he said, "for a woman to be beating her own daughter. I am asking you now the why of it?"

All three waited for the widow's answer, and when it came the words tumbled from her. " 'Tis sad entirely I am, to be beating the lass. But she has me troubled entirely by all the work she does. I beat her from the spinning and she takes to the weaving; I beat her from the weaving and she takes to the knitting; I beat . . ."

Here the King of Ireland's son spoke: " 'Tis enough said. For a year and a day I have been riding the length and width of Ireland, searching for the prettiest lass who can work the best in the land. For my mother, the Queen, will never be letting me marry a lazy girl. So if it's all the same to you, my good woman, I'll be taking the lass to the castle, and marrying her on the morrow."

He lifted Eileen upon the saddle in front of him. Then he reached in his pocket and brought out a small bag of gold. Throwing it to the widow, he said, " 'Twill pay somewhat for the loss of your daughter." With that he put spurs to the white horse and the two of them were off, the wind at their back and luck following after.

When they reached the castle the Queen met them at the door. "Here is a lass after your own heart, Mother. She is the hardest worker in all of Ireland, and the prettiest as well. What better wife can the King of Ireland's son have? Tell me that!"

The Queen looked hard and long at Eileen—at her rags, at her bare feet, and at the wildness of her hair. "She is pretty, that I grant you. But she has not the look of a lass that can work. What can she do?"

"She can spin, weave, knit —"

"Whose word did you take for it?"

"Whose but her mother's!"

The Queen shook a sorry head. "Lad, lad, you've been foolish entirely. What mother in the whole world would say but the best of her daughter?"

"But I caught her at the crossroads, beating the lass. And for why? Because she would never give over her working."

"Maybe she was beating her because she would never begin. You may well have fetched me the laziest girl in all of Ireland. Set her down from the saddle and we'll let her sleep the night. On the morrow we will give her a fair test of the work."

That night Eileen slept in a gold bed with sheets of satin under and over her. With the first of the sun the Queen woke her. "Come! You'll have your fill of tea, stirabout and griddle bread. Then you'll be put to the spinning."

Her hunger gone, Eileen was led down a long, long corridor to a small room. Inside stood a spinning wheel and stool. Along the walls were piled stacks of flax, carded and ready. "You'll spin that flax into fine linen thread the day." With that the Queen was gone, and the door locked after her.

Eileen sat down on the stool. For the first time in her life, the shame of her laziness took her.

Deep she buried her face in her hands. Good for
nothing she was. It mattered little now that the
lad she loved was the King's son, that he lived in
a castle, with plenty and to spare. She would lose
him this day—that was all that mattered. Heavy,
heavy hung the burden of that loss on her heart,
and she wept—as she had never wept before.

A gentle tapping came at the window. Eileen
rubbed the tears from her eyes, the better to see.
There on the other side of the window stood a
small woman in green, with a wee red bonnet on
her head. She was tapping for the girl to let her
in. Eileen sprang to her feet and opened the window. Down from the sill jumped the wee woman.
"For why are you weeping, Eileen?" she asked.

"All my life I have been the laziest girl in all
of Ireland. All my life I have let my poor mother
work for me. Now because I cannot spin, or
weave, or knit—I'll not be let marry the King's
son."

"And you love him?" asked the wee woman.

"I love him—were he naught but a tinker on the road, with never a house to hold him or a rag to cover him."

"If you will make me a promise, and keep it, I'll spin the flax for you the day."

"I will make you any promise and keep it," cried the girl.

" 'Tis a bargain," said the wee woman. And she took from under the cape that she wore a wee spinning wheel, with a stool to match it. She told Eileen to fetch over bundles of the flax. Putting a foot on the treadle, she took an end of the flax and fastened it to the spindle. The wheel started its humming and above the humming the wee woman set a tune to the whirling of the wheel— and what she sang was this:

> *"Turn wheel, turn about,*
> *Spin flax, spin.*
> *Reel, reel, faster reel,*
> *Out and in.*

Laugh, laugh, Fairies laugh,
When this is done—
I wish me at the wedding
Of the King's own son."

When the song ended, all the flax was spun and hundreds of bobbins of fine linen thread lay stacked in the room's corner.

"Don't you be forgetting, Eileen," said the wee woman, and like a wisp of green smoke she was out of the window and gone.

At day's end the Queen came. She counted the bobbins in the corner. Her fingers felt the fineness and smoothness of the thread. She gave the girl a bit of smile as she said, "I see you can spin. We'll be seeing can you weave, on the morrow."

That night the girl sat at the royal table and ate her fill. Only once did she lift her eyes to the King's son, letting the full of her love shine in them. " 'Tis a loving lass as well as a pretty one," thought he. "What matters if she can spin and weave!"

On the morrow when the Queen took the girl to the small room there stood a loom and a bench for the weaver, with a shuttle resting on it. "You'll wind the shuttle and begin," said the

Queen. "If every bobbin is not empty at the end of the day, and the room holding lengths of fine linen cloth, you'll not be let marry my son." With that she was gone, the door locked after her.

The girl sat, thinking again of the shame of her laziness, her head buried in her two hands. What roused her was the sound of tapping at the window. When she looked, there stood another wee woman all in green and a red bonnet on her wee head. She was beckoning to the girl to let her in. Eileen sprang to her feet and opened the window. In a thrice the wee woman was down to the floor, asking, "For why are you weeping, Eileen?"

The same answer came to the girl's tongue: "All my life I have been the laziest girl in all of Ireland. All my life I have let my poor mother work for me. And now—because I cannot weave, or knit—I'll never be let marry the King's son."

"And do you love him, Eileen?"

"I love him till my heart is near broken, thinking of the long years ahead without him."

"If you will make me a promise, and keep it, I'll be weaving the fine linen for you this day."

"I will make you any promise and keep it," said the girl.

" 'Tis a bargain," said the wee woman and she took out from under the cape that covered her a wee loom and a bench to match. From a pocket she took out a wee silver shuttle. "Fetch me the bobbins from the room's corner," said she. She wound the shuttle and she tied the first thread. She sat herself on the bench and put her feet to the treadles. She threw her shuttle and set her song to the click of the treadles. This is what she sang:

"Fly shuttle, faster fly,
　　Weave firm and strong,
Roll linen on the bolt
　　While I lilt my song.
Laugh, laugh, Fairies laugh,
　　When this is done,
I wish me at the wedding
　　Of the King's own son."

With the end of the song, every bobbin was empty. Between them Eileen and the wee woman folded the lengths of fine linen and laid them tidily upon the floor. In the flicker of a lash, the wee woman was on the sill and out the window. But as she went she said to the girl, "Don't you be forgetting, Eileen."

There came the turn of the key in the lock, the opening of the door, and there stood the Queen. It took her no time at all, to see the empty bobbins and the linen woven and folded. She felt of the weave and marked the smooth-finished edge of each fold. Then she gave the girl more than half of a smile. "You can spin; you can weave. Can you knit now? We'll be trying you at it, come the morrow."

On the morrow the Queen took the girl to the small room. This time it was stacked high with skeins of yarn. She gave Eileen a pair of golden knitting needles. "You'll have all the yarn knit by day's end, or back to your mother you go." And with that the Queen was gone and the door locked behind her.

Long sat the widow's lazy daughter, making a sobbing-place of her heart. It had taken her mother more than half of a week to knit a pair of stockings—and she at it the lee-long day. The girl knew it would take a mortal lass more than a year and a day to knit into stockings the stack of yarn filling the room. She buried her face deep in her hands and wept as she had never wept before.

Again the sound of tapping roused her. A third wee wee fairy-woman in a green cape and red bonnet beckoned her to let her in.

It happened with the third as it had happened with the others. She asked:

"For why are you weeping, Eileen?"

And for the third time the girl made answer. "All my life I have been the laziest girl in Ireland, letting my poor mother do all the work. And now —because I cannot knit—I'll not be let marry the King's son."

"If you will make me a promise, and keep it, I will knit the yarn for you."

"I will make any promise and I'll keep it!" cried the girl.

" 'Tis a bargain entirely," said the wee woman. She took a creepy-stool from under her cape and from her pocket she took a wee pair of silver knitting needles. Down she sat; and drawing to her a pile of the green skeins, she twisted a free end of yarn around her wee finger.

The next moment the needles were filling the small room with their clicking. So fast moved the wee woman's fingers that they made a blur before the girl's eyes like the quivering wings of a honey-bird; and as she knit she sang:

"Knit, knit, needles click
 Work fast today,
Stockings all on line must be
 Before I'm away.
Laugh, laugh, Fairies laugh,
 When this is done
I wish me at the wedding
 Of the King's own son."

With the end of the song, there were more than a hundred pairs of stockings on the line. Wonderment held the girl, and never a word could she speak.

The wee woman was out of the window in a thrice saying to the girl, "Don't you be forgetting, Eileen."

With the end of the day came the Queen. She looked at the stockings. She counted the pairs. For the first time since the girl had entered the castle gate the Queen smiled the whole of her heart at her.

"In faith, you must be the best worker in all of Ireland, for you have done what no mortal hands could do. Come! On the morrow we make ready for the feast and the wedding."

The great and the grand of Ireland were asked to the wedding. Eileen wore a dress of white gossamer that had the look of moonbeams spun around her. Her veil was the finest of Irish lace; and she wore a wee golden crown on her head. After the bishop's blessing, she sat down at the royal table—between the King and the King's son.

The great feasting hall was filled, saving three empty chairs close to the royal table.

"Let the feasting begin!" cried the King. But at that very moment there came a knocking, low down, on the great door. A serving man opened it—and who should come in but a wee small woman in a green cape and a red bonnet. Every eye saw as she came down the hall that one of the wee woman's feet was enormous—ten times the size it should have been.

The King rose. "Who bid you to the wedding?"

The wee woman looked at Eileen, "I am a guest —bidden by the bride."

"Is that the truth?" asked the King.

The girl nodded. " 'Tis the binding truth."

The King waved his hand to one of the empty seats. "Sit you down and welcome, wee woman that you are. But however did you come by that one monstrous foot?"

The wee woman laughed—and it made the

sound of joyful bells to Eileen. "I have been spinning for hundreds of years. 'Tis the long pressing
of the foot to the treadle that has made it grow."

The King's son spoke: "If that is what comes
from the spinning, I will never let my bride spin
again."

There came another knocking at the door.
When the servant man opened it, in stepped another wee woman in a green cape and a red bonnet. She came down the hall, straight for the
second empty seat. As she came everyone saw the
long length of both of her arms. So long they
were the fingers touched the ground as she walked.

The King spoke: "Who bid you come to the
wedding?"

"Who but the bride?"

"Is that the truth?" asked the King.

"Aye, 'tis the binding truth," said the girl.

"Sit you down," said the King. "But first, tell
me how you came by those monstrous long arms
of yours?"

"For hundreds of years I have been weaving,"
said the wee woman. "'Tis the throwing of the
shuttle back and forth—back and forth—that has
made them grow longer."

"Aii!" said the King's son. "If that is what
comes of it, I'll never let my bride weave again."

For the third time came the knocking. All who
watched saw that the third woman had a monstrous great nose."

"Tell me," said the King, "how you came by that
nose?"

"For hundreds of years I have been knitting.
And always I have been holding the needles

closer and closer—till they've hit the nose hour after hour and it has grown longer and fatter and redder as it is now."

"Aii!" said the King's son. "If that is what comes of knitting, I will never let my bride knit again." He laughed as full and hearty as the wee woman, and placed a kiss on the tip of Eileen's nose. "By this and by that, I am thinking it's not a working bride we need at all in the castle, but a pretty one. And that we have!"

The Queen looked hard at the two of them, and said too softly for aught but the King to hear, "And I am thinking that a bride who has the blessing of the fairy people is better than one who can spin, or weave, or knit."

Patrick O'Donnell and the Leprechaun

PATRICK O'DONNELL was coming home one night from the county fair in Donegal. He was taking the rise in the road when he heard off in the bogland a shrill wee cry.

Said he to himself, " 'Tis not the cry of a wee one and 'tis not the cry of a creature caught in the furze. I will go and have a look."

So over the bog he stepped, passing one black thornbush after another, for the bog was full of them. And he came at last to the thornbush that was holding the cry.

Now there was a moon in the sky and the skies were bright, so he could see what was there. He could see to his wonderment a wee fairy man hung by the seat of his breeches on a long black thorn. He stepped closer now and asked, "How did you get yourself in this plight, wee small man that you are?"

With that he knocked his foot on something small on the ground and he looked below. There he saw a wee cobbler's bench with pegs and bits of leather and with all the things of a cobbler's trade.

"Aha," he said aloud to himself and the wee man. " 'Tis a leprechaun you are, wee man."

The leprechaun had stopped his squealing, and now he spoke with great impatience. "It's a small matter if I am. Take me off the blackthorn, where I'm likely to die if you don't. And take great care that you do not tear my breeches, for they are a new pair."

You can well believe that Patrick O'Donnell was filled with more than wonderment now, for he knew that the leprechaun was safe in his hands. He could ask where the crock of fairy gold was hidden, and the leprechaun by all the laws of fairy trade was bound to tell him.

So, with great care, he took the wee man by the scruff of his neck and the seat of his breeches

and gently lifted him free of the blackthorn.

"Put me fast to the earth," said the wee man.

"I will not," said Patrick. "'Tis a leprechaun you are and 'tis on you I'll keep my hands and my eyes until you'll be after telling me where the pot of gold is hid."

"Have a heart," said the wee man. "What is a pot of gold to you?"

" 'Tis the making of my family fortune," said Patrick O'Donnell, "and without it I am thinking we'll never have one."

There followed a long time with nought but blathering between them. In the end, with his hands still fast on the seat of his breeches and the scruff of his neck, Patrick O'Donnell went across the bog as the leprechaun directed, until they came to a certain blackthorn bush.

" 'Tis here it is hid," said the leprechaun, sounding sad.

"Are you sure?" asked Patrick O'Donnell.

"I'm as sure of it as that I am the wee man

who mends all the fairies' shoes after their dancing. Dig under that blackthorn yonder, and
you'll find the fairies' gold."

Patrick O'Donnell looked about him under the
starlight at all the blackthorn bushes on the bog
and he shook his head with great hopelessness.

"I have no spade at all to dig with," said he,
"and if I go home for it, how will I find which
bush it is when I come back?"

"That's a trouble that's all your own," said the
wee fairy man. With that a great silence fell
between them.

It was Patrick himself that broke it.

"I have the answer," said he, sending up a great
shout. "I'll tie my bright kerchief to the bush,
and even by the starlight, dark as it is, I'll be able
to tell which bush holds the crock of gold."

The fairy man set up a great chuckling. "Tie
your kerchief fast now, and leave us both be going our ways."

Patrick, now sure of his family's fortune, let

the leprechaun go. Whisht! Like a shooting star in the night, he vanished, while Patrick untied the kerchief from about his neck and tied it fast to the blackthorn bush.

It took him the rest of the night to reach home and find himself a stout spade, and then tramp down to the bog again.

The bright orange of the sunrise was making a ring for the new day around the sky when he started across the bog. It made bright every patch of grass and stubble, furze and bush, as he tramped.

He was half across the bog when he looked about. To his great bewilderment he saw that every thornbush around him had a bright kerchief tied to it, the same as he had tied to the thornbush the leprechaun had shown him.

"If I should live to be a hundred," said Patrick O'Donnell, "I could never dig up the whole of them." So there was the ending of the O'Donnell fortune.